REFLECTIONS

RECOLLECTIONS

REVELATIONS

VOLUME ONE

REFLECTIONS
RECOLLECTIONS
REVELATIONS

VOLUME ONE

a

Collection of

Inspirational Short Stories

Reflections, Recollections, Revelations
A Collection of Inspirational Short Stories
Volume One

© 2018 by Linda R. Sutton

Cover Design by Jeff Taylor/Linda Sutton

Unless otherwise indicated, Scripture quotations are from the King James Version of the Bible (KJV)

ISBN 978-1-7322187-0-3

DEDICATION

I dedicate this book in memory of my Dad who always loved and taught me to love.

This work is also dedicated in memory of Mrs. Maggie J. Bass, "my other mother." We shared a heartfelt love and I always knew she understood the person of me.

CONTENTS

Works from Contributing Writers

Foreword

From time to time no matter how deep or how anointed we may be, if we're not careful we can find ourselves drifting off course. This may not be a physical thing, but an awareness that we can be in church or in Bible study, but just going through the motions. If I find myself in that space, I've observed that my spirit and emotions can shift, and I begin to experience tension in my relationships with people and sometimes even with God. I know many people don't want to acknowledge that, but it can happen to anyone. You still show up and you still love God, but you feel a little off track – like your faith is being challenged.

It's a random, vague place where we are trying to make sense of life, and trying to make sense of where we are in certain seasons of life. I don't know about you, but I recognize that I need God to do something and I need HIM to do it fast because it seems that I am under attack on every hand. I come to the realization that the adversary has strategically launched an attack upon my life to uproot and discourage me. I have even found myself struggling to know if I will ever come out of those situations and yet, I always do.

Perhaps you are reading this today and you can testify that at your highest point, HE was there. I'm sure there are some who can testify that at the lowest point, HE was still there. Through all the highs, the lows, the ups and yes, the downs, HE was there all the time! Through losing jobs and falling on hard times, through changes in relationships and rearing children, through paying bills and starting companies, through relocating to another state and going back to school – God kept reminding you that HE was right there. Even when you were going through asking God, *"How long?"* – HE WAS THERE!

HE was there on the day when everything that COULD go wrong DID go wrong: you woke up and burned your breakfast; spilled coffee on your shirt; burned the print of the iron onto your jacket; your babies have a bad day and throw temper tantrums; your dog threw up; your goldfish died; and you get outside only to realize you have a flat tire! And if that's not enough, you finally get to work and they are upset because you were late. But in the midst of chaos on every hand, you get the reassurance of that still small voice saying, *"I'm right here. You do not have to go through what you are going through by yourself."*

Aren't you grateful for how He reminds us in every season and at every place in our life that He will never leave us nor forsake us, but He will be right there?

You are about to embark upon a journey of short stories that collectively serve as reminders that no matter WHO you are, WHERE you are, or WHAT you may be going through, you are not alone. God is right there with you! Not only is HE right there with you, HE is there to deliver you and give you peace.

About Linda

I actually can't remember when I first met Linda Sutton. She is one of those individuals that I can't remember ever *not* knowing. We've been fellow church members on the pew, and now she's a member of the congregation that I serve as pastor. On every level, she has been a joy to know. To observe her quiet spirit and peaceful presence, most would never know the fires she's had to endure and the trials she's experienced in order to prepare her for the expression of this work and those to come. Linda does a masterful job of sharing her own personal reflections and observations of God's faithfulness with a transparency that is both rare and refreshing. Her stories are captivating and her songs of deliverance will continue to echo throughout the corridors of your mind long after you have placed this volume back on the shelf.

As I read the book, I smiled with a Godly pride and cheered like a mother in the stands at a sporting event to see and read "the work" that God had done through a willing vessel. This collection will be a welcomed addition to your personal library and one that you will want to read over and over again.

I introduce to some and present to others from a daughter of the house and a dear woman of God whom I rejoice to call friend, the first of the many literary works of LINDA ROSE SUTTON.

Jennifer R. Biard

Jennifer R. Biard, Senior Pastor
Jackson Revival Center Church, Inc. | Jackson, MS

Preface

Sharing this work has been a journey of joy, and I've encountered some lovely surprises along the way. It was only after the work had been completed and in the process of going to print that I found a Prophetic Word that had been spoken, typed and given to me in October, 2003. Somehow, it had been placed in a "to be filed" folder and left there for years. While in search for another document, it was found. It is included here as testament to the power of God to bring His Word to pass. God does say in Isaiah 55:11 *So shall my word be that goeth forth out of my mouth; it shall not return unto me void, but it shall accomplish that which I please, and it shall prosper in the thing whereto I sent it.* Praise God! Though it has taken all these many years, God is faithful that promised. I'm ever amazed at His working in my life.

As spoken to me on October 1, 2003, The Prophetic Word:

> *Begin to write memoirs (autobiography/ life experiences, revelation knowledge of God's word and such). The Word will continue to bring forth life in the hearts and lives of my people. Build up the Body of Christ to the glory of God. Even as the body of a dead man fell on the bones of Elijah and sprang forth life, so shall it be with the words of life that you shall even for the written pages of that which I shall instruct you to write. It shall spring*

forth life to those that appear dead in the days to come, that you might give me glory not only in life but in the life to come. I will make your hand as one with the pen of a ready writer. Hear and write that which you hear and all that I will reveal and even have already revealed. This is a work that I desire of thee to bring me glory. I will complete and finish the work of your hands as you write. Do not hesitate, nor detain.

Introduction

In the pursuit of completing my first work, *Prayers, Praises and Poetic Phrases*, I felt God's nudging to embark upon yet another publication. He so impressed in my spirit to share my personal experiences giving witness to the power of His Living Word. There was a sense of urgency within me to "get it done." I felt His stirring and gladly gave myself to this endeavor that others might be inspired, encouraged and strengthened in their faith journey. In doing so, I knew He was breathing life into the words that would be seen and read of men. Each day, He gave divine inspiration and I was ready with excitement to pour out as He poured in. Let me tell you, the Spirit of God made me to understand that during this journey of writing I had to lend myself to be positioned with three things:

A Hearing Ear

A Listening Heart

and the Pen of a Ready Writer

What a beautiful journey it has been and continues to be. As I pressed forward with the work, some distractions and hindrances were encountered. However, not to be denied, these only served to fuel me with the fortitude to finish and press print. Hallelujah! To God be the glory!

Thoughts that stirred my being have been penned in this collection of inspirational stories—life experiences that warm the heart and soul. These *Reflections, Recollections, Revelations* are now printed on the pages of this book as expressions of the heart, life lessons taught and joys realized. They are accounts that attest to the love and power of God. They are written to stimulate one to ponder and thought; to give reason for pause and reflection.

Perhaps you might find yourself somewhere in the pages of this book. My prayer is that these writings will minister and breathe life into you; that you will be refreshed, renewed and blessed. More importantly, it is my prayer that souls will be stirred to receive Jesus Christ as Lord and Savior. And, yes, while you are receiving all of that, be sure to "enjoy" the reading.

Humbly Submitted,
Linda R. Sutton

Daddy's Driving

We spent a lot of time traveling during my growing up years. There was a week in and week out ritual that we all knew quite well. You see, we attended school where my parents worked during the week—which happened to be my mom's hometown, and then on weekends we traveled about 70 or 80 miles away to attend church in my dad's hometown.

The six of us children would load up in the camper on the back of the truck and on our way we'd go. With daddy driving, we would start out and many times it didn't take long before we would burst out in a joyous chorus of church songs that we all knew. That helped to make the travel time shorter. My dad was always driving, you see, because my mom didn't learn to drive until us children were well up in age and even then she just let my dad do all the driving. I can remember many trips when the ride seemed to lull me to sleep. But in reflection, I'm convinced it was more so the thought that my dad was driving, and I knew we were all in safe hands. He knew the way, and we all could trust him to watch out and protect us from dangers along the journey. He had a watchful eye and a care that we could depend on. A father does that. And just think how much more our Heavenly Father cares for us, provides for us, loves us, and indeed watches over us each and every day as we travel the twists and turns, the dangerous curves of life's road, in the heat of the day or darkness of the night all along life's journey. We could rest assured we were safe when daddy was driving. He knew the way and how to get us safely to our destination. Somehow, when the truck stopped, I knew we had arrived safely to our destination. Of course, today's technology has so evolved that we trust in it to direct the way, but there is just nothing like a father's love that we know, feel, and rest in when He's at the wheel.

The Blind Side

I can remember as a young child riding along the country road to my grandparents' house. The road was curvy with some steep hills. But one hill seemed especially high. Every time we would go up and over that hill, it seemed as if my heart would sink to the pit of my stomach. There was a bit of fear and joy all at the same time. Even today, there is a steep hill—and I do mean steep hill, that I sometimes travel to a friend's home that goes up to an almost vertical position where you are blind to what's on the downside of the hill. Though I have driven many times slowly and carefully over this hill, I'm still uneasy about the downside.

As it is in life's journeys, we must trust God in what we can see as well as what we cannot see. That's faith, and we must have faith to please God. *But without faith it is impossible to please Him: for he that cometh to God must believe that He is, and that He is a rewarder of them that diligently seek Him* as so written in Hebrews 11:6.

There was one definition of faith shared in a church service many years ago that so witnessed and resonated with me. Simply stated, faith is "trusting all that you know about God to lead you to a safe landing." God is omnipotent, omniscient and omnipresent. He knows and sees all. He does not have a blind side. We can be assured of God's care and keeping. No matter the steepest way up any hill or how blind the downside, activate your faith. Trust God!

Grace Accounts

It was though as the old folks used to say "I had lost my ever loving mind." No, it wasn't as if I wasn't taught and didn't know any better. What happen was, I just let my flesh overrule my sense, my spiritual understanding. Now, I know you know what I'm talking about. You know the times when you know better, but you just don't do better. Those times can bring you to some wilderness experiences. But thank God for his love, grace and mercy, that never gives up on us and never leaves us even in the midst of our mess. His heart is towards us even though we falter. Yes, even when we then seek to hide as Adam and Eve did in the Garden or as Jonah did in the ship and ultimately ended up in the whale's belly.

Psalm 139 gives us such a beautiful hope in the mercies of the all-knowing God. The questions are posed in verse 7, *Whither shall I go from thy spirit? or whither shall I flee from thy presence?* We come to understand that Our Father God is omniscient, omnipotent and omnipresent. There may be points in our lives where we lose sight of the plan, purpose, and pursuit to which we are called and become entangled, ensnared or entwined with vines as Jonah was in the whale or err in disobedience to God's Word and attempt to find cover as Adam and Eve did. But we don't have to stay in a fallen state. We don't have to feel that we have wandered too far or messed up too bad. We are neither hopeless nor helpless.

Remember I said that God is omnipresent. And just as He is all-knowing, His love is unconditional. His love is more than amazing! His love for us is past finding out! We cannot understand it! We simply receive His love. We repent where we falter and receive His forgiveness as we walk in forgiveness. I John 2:1 sheds this understanding on God's grace as it is written, *My little children, these things write I unto you, that ye sin not. And if any man sin, we have an advocate with the Father, Jesus Christ the righteous.* Receive the blood of Jesus that was shed for the atonement of our sins past, present and future. We are covered when we repent and the desire of our heart is to be restored, to walk in right standing and in fellowship with God.

We've heard said, "No one is perfect" and Ecclesiastes 7:20 affirms, *For there is not a just man upon earth, that doeth good, and sinneth not.* Whether in thought, word, or deed, it happens; we experience missteps in our walk of faith. Don't despair in errs, don't remain in the pain of failures, don't be distraught in faults. Draw on the grace account availed to us and commit to live life pleasing unto God so that we can freely worship, praise, and have fellowship with Him.

The Present

Each day as we awaken to unwrap the present of today, may we experience the awe and wonder as on Christmas Morn. May our hearts fill with joy and thanksgiving for His tender love and care, and may we cherish His thoughts towards us to give hope and a future.

As we remove the wrapping on His present for us today, let our hearts trust His wisdom in the giving of the gift. Know that it's the good and perfect gift, being completely certain that its unique design and selection has us in mind. He knows what's best. Though we may not understand it, believe with childlike faith that all is working for good, just the way He said. Let us ever praise Him and render due glory and honor to His Name.

Always remember that yesterdays are all past. We have lived; we have learned to be more the wiser. Be mindful that He's made the way for "all forgiven" as likewise we must do. Receive the unblemished present of each new today and ever pray that He keeps us lest we stray.

So as we begin the present of today anew, receive the gift with gratitude. Render praise and worship as to say, "O Lord, my soul loves you." Let's give our heart in sweet surrender to His Will, His Way, His Word. For His ever present presence, let us all say, "Amen and Amen."

Early Seekers

At a place of pause from doing life with the usual work routine, I looked forward to awakening and spending more time with the Father God in prayer, praise, worship and His Word. It was the early time when my mind and body were fresh from the rest of the night and my thoughts were not cluttered with daily "to do" lists for the affairs of life. Those mornings I so enjoyed and emerged refreshed, renewed and inspired by God's Spirit for what the day would unfold. I found those early mornings with God to be sweet, quiet and filled with His peace and His presence; mornings that are still enough for your spirit to soar as you listen to the sweet serenade of birds chirping, as you breathe in and smell the freshness of the new day, as you see the diamond sparkle of the sun's rays as it begins to make itself known upon the earth, and you have an awesome awareness of God's majesty, glory and power. Those moments are to be cherished for it's there you can enter into the secret places that only God's spirit can take you; it's there that you can learn of Him and experience that which mere words cannot express. In the hustle and bustle of this world, ask God to help you put purpose in place for first fellowship with the Father before beginning each day anew. Note the words of Proverbs 8:17, *I love them that love me; and those that seek me early shall find me.*

Let me interject here, there is something to be said for the midnight warriors, the midnight watchmen and gatekeepers. I've had my time there too. It's a rewarding time where we often find miracles birthed. It was the midnight hour that Acts 16:25-27 records, *And at midnight Paul and Silas prayed, and sang praises unto God: and the prisoners heard them. And suddenly there was a great earthquake, so that the foundations of the prison were shaken: and immediately all the doors were opened, and every one's bands were loosed.* Acts 12:5 records that, *Peter therefore was kept in prison; but prayer was made without ceasing of the church unto God for him.* As Peter slept that night an angel of the Lord came, a light shined in that prison, those chains fell off Peter and he was led out of that prison where the gate to the city opened and he walked right on down to that Church Prayer Meeting and stood knocking at the door. Talk about a miracle. Whether an early seeker or a midnight warrior, know that spending time before God is always good and always needed.

Fueled Up

A vehicle will inevitably stop in its tracks if ever it runs out of gas. That can be a rather embarrassing, frustrating and alarming experience for anyone. Just as we must refill our vehicle tanks with fuel to keep moving along, so must we do with our natural and spiritual man. When it comes to our natural bodies, statistics seem to show that in our nation most are sure to keep the flesh well replenished.

Our spirit man has the need to be renewed and refreshed as well. We cannot run on fumes and be effective in this faith journey. There's a daily need to come to the filling station to be refilled and recharged so that we are refreshed in our spirit, our soul and our mind.

The Father has called us as able ministers, as disciples, as witnesses for Him in the earth. Each day we pour out to others whether in the sanctuary, the home, the workplace, the city, the field, the highway or the byway. As we pour out to others, we must be poured into so that we don't find ourselves running on fumes. 2 Timothy 2:15 admonishes us to *Study to shew thyself approved unto God, a workman that needeth not to be ashamed, rightly dividing the word of truth.* Jude 1:20 prevails upon us, *But ye, beloved, building up yourselves on your most holy faith, praying in the Holy Ghost...* Each day as we apply ourselves to knowledge and wisdom in God's Word, as we commune with Him in prayer and meditation, we receive manna that sustains and fuels us to move forward on the given path.

As God fed the Israelites new manna each day, so His mercies are new every morning for us. Lamentations 3:22-23 reminds us *It is of the Lord's mercies that we are not consumed, because His compassions fail not. They are new every morning: great is Thy faithfulness.* Jesus taught the disciples to pray, *Give us this day our daily bread* as Matthew 6:11 records. It's daily that we are to come before God's throne of grace and mercy to make our requests known and seek His will. It's there we receive of His hand, of His spirit which fuels our faith to power on.

Jesus told His disciples many parables. In Luke 18:1 we read, *And He spake a parable unto them to this end, that men ought always to pray, and not faint...* We understand that Jesus, Our Lord and Savior withdrew from the multitude to pray and communed with The Father always. How much more must we do so for our sufficiency? We must take time to pull aside and refuel.

Psalm 100:4 says *Enter into His gates with thanksgiving, and into His courts with praise...* Enter into His Holy presence and allow Him to refuel, refresh, and renew. Spend time there in Holy Communion for Psalm 16:11 tells us that *Thou wilt shew me the path of life: in thy presence is fullness of joy; at thy right hand there are pleasures for evermore.* As referenced in Nehemiah 8:10... *for the joy of the Lord is your strength.* Have you been by the filling station today?

Light and Shade

In life, it is said for every action there is an equal and opposite reaction. With love, there's hate; for life, there's death; good versus evil; what goes up, must come down; we breathe in, we breathe out; we give and we take; we hold on to or we let go of—the light and shade of it all goes on and on. It could be proposed here that while these equal and opposite reactions may take us to the extremes of the spectrum, that they also bring us to the place of understanding the need for balance.

As I thought more on this, I began to consider this idea as it relates to the kingdom of God. While not embarking on a scientific discussion and discovery mission here, let's just explore the thought of hot and cold. Here on planet earth we experience both. Let's imagine a world without the sun, the source of heat. The implications of such an extreme might very well be a question of survival, so might such a world without the Son of God, our Lord and Savior, Jesus Christ. When we think of fallen mankind without our Redeemer, the implications are dire.

Again, imagine a world upon which judgment and justice was pronounced without mercy. But praise

God for His love, His Grace, His Mercy. It was God, Our Father that... *so loved the world, that He gave His only begotten Son, that whosoever believeth in Him should not perish, but have everlasting life,* as recorded in John 3:16. It was Jesus, His only begotten Son who balanced it all for us on the cross where God's justice and mercy met. Psalm 85:10 records that *Mercy and truth are met together; righteousness and peace have kissed each other.* Let all say, "Yes and Amen." Hallelujah! Glory Be To God!

Capture The Moment

The Spirit of God gives us moments in our lives that we experience light and revelation of His Word that we otherwise might not know. I Corinthians 2:14 clearly states, *But the natural man receiveth not the things of the Spirit of God: for they are foolishness unto him: neither can he know them, because they are spiritually discerned.* At those moments of God's present visitation, our minds receive understanding and insight to the hidden things of God. We do well to seize those moments, take note, write down, ask the Holy Spirit to inscribe it upon the tables of our heart that those precious revelations from God do not become lost treasure or simply a dissipating moment in time.

The Heavenly Father is so gracious to give us just such a moment(s). Our priority should always be to stop and listen. The scripture records experiences like that as Paul describes his visions and revelations of the Lord in 2 Corinthians 12. He tells of one caught up to the third heaven and in Verse 3-4 continues, *And I knew such a man, (whether in the body, or out of the body, I cannot tell: God knoweth;) How that he was caught up into paradise, and heard unspeakable words, which it is not lawful for a man to utter.* The disciples so desired understanding and inquired of Jesus to expound and explain the meaning of the parables spoken to the multitudes. Jesus did so in the gospels of Matthew, Mark, and Luke and told them that it was given unto them to know the mysteries of the Kingdom of Heaven. We read in the Book of Revelation that John... *was in the isle that is called Patmos, for the Word of God, and for the testimony of Jesus Christ. I was in the Spirit on the Lord's day, and heard behind me a great voice, as of a trumpet, Saying, I am Alpha and Omega, the first and the last:* and, *What thou seest, write in a book...* referenced in Chapter 1:9-11. I remember my Senior Pastor in his time sharing that in just such a moment that the Spirit of God seemed to open up the Bible, His Holy Word unto him and in that moment He understood the scriptures.

When you sense the Spirit of God speaking to you, Stop, Listen and Receive. This might just be your moment, the moment you have been waiting for that gives you the Key to unlock that which you have long awaited, prayed and sought God for. Don't let this moment pass you by. We do understand that the adversary will try to steal that moment, that Word, but give no place, no room for it. Let your mind only be open and your face set as a flint towards the things of God to hear, to know, to experience, to live. Set your affection on things above.

As Christians, God's Spirit abides in us and so desires to give us those moments as we spend time and delight ourselves in Him. We are admonished in Psalm 37:4-5 to *Delight thyself also in the Lord: and*

He shall give thee the desires of thine heart. Commit thy way unto the Lord; trust also in Him; and He shall bring it to pass. We read further in Isaiah 26:3 that, *Thou will keep him in perfect peace, whose mind is stayed on thee: because he trusteth in thee.* Keep walking in Faith. Keep listening for His Voice. When He Speaks, Stop and "Capture the Moment." Don't let it escape you! It's a treasure to be cherished and will enrich your total being, taking you to deeper depths and higher heights in Him. Praise God! What a glorious place to be if only but for a moment.

Date Night

Sometimes I wonder whatever happened to the days of planned "together time." You know, the days of romance where we made the time to write love notes or texts, to give or send flowers, to find and present that perfect card or "just because" gift—better yet, a planned date night doing some fun activity that was God approved, of course.

Maybe that was just a figment of my imagination. But I was pleasantly surprised during a conversation with a young lady that I met in a store while checking out. We were scheduling a call back for the next day when she informed me to call before 4 p.m. She explained that she and her husband always had a planned date night on Thursdays. At 4 p.m. everything else came to a stop, and their together time started. My hope in romance was renewed. It was so refreshing to meet someone that realized the need and put forth the effort towards spending quality time cultivating and sustaining a relationship.

As I reveled in the lovely thought of date night, my heart began to envision the special time of communion with my God. So vividly I can remember the days He wooed me, drawing me close, yet closer still by the wonder of His unconditional love. The fragrance lingers on from the beautiful bouquet of flowers He brings me spring, winter, summer and fall. Cherished are those "just because" gifts He sends me by the special messenger of His Holy Spirit. My heart melts when I read and re-read the many letters He has written always telling His love for me. What lovely invitations He has given me to dine and taste of His goodness. The table He sets before me ever leaves me in awe. My soul is always refreshed on the long walks He takes me, while His heart He shares and glorious secrets impart. He takes my breath away each time He sweeps me gently up into His arms and carries me so that I might rest awhile. My heart knows sheer joy for the times of sweet communion while sitting at His feet. My spirit soars as He takes me to a place of the divine, where a bit of heaven on earth I find. With great anticipation, I relish the thought of our moments together, and not just for date night, but life full and filled basking in His presence.

He Gets Me

Recently, I was pleasantly surprised and delighted to receive an e-mail message from a dear friend extending greetings. The e-mail included an attachment that when opened blossomed into a beautiful yellow rose. That simple act so touched my heart. Not only was it beautiful, but it was my favorite flower in my favorite color. Simple acts of kindness when we take the time to reach out can uplift, encourage and just bring a smile to someone's face. My wonder in this act of kindness, however, was how this friend knew my favorite flower and my favorite color because this was something that had not been revealed. There are times in life with our complicated selves that we may think no one understands us, no one knows how we feel, no one sees who we are or no one cares. No one "Gets Us." To the contrary, we who are "fearfully and wonderfully made" can be assured that the creator of our being knows us through and through. He knew us even in our mother's womb just as recounted in Jeremiah 1:4-5, *Then the word of the Lord came unto me, saying, before I formed thee in the belly I knew thee; and before thou camest out of the womb I sanctified thee...*

Psalm 139 speaks to the all-knowing God knowing all of us. It begins, *O Lord, thou has searched me, and known me. Thou knowest my downsitting and mine uprising, thou understandest my thought afar off.* It continues... *For there is not a word in my tongue, but, lo, O Lord, thou knowest it altogether...*

God knows the deepest longings of our hearts. We all want to be understood, to be cared for, to be loved. When that happens, it's fulfilling to the core of our being, to our soul. It is a wonderful moment of joy when you realize that someone "Gets You." Meditate today on God's love for you, His care of you and knowing that "He Gets You." Say this to yourself, "God Gets Me because He begot Me."

Just Because

At times we just need to be embraced, to feel and know love. We desire and welcome a caring touch, a gentle hug, a delightful greeting, a warm smile or an encouraging text. Acts of kindness shown might well be that which gives someone hope for tomorrow. It might be the difference between life and death or it can be the sunshine in someone's day. As Christians, we are to show love in action because that's what we do by the grace of God. God is love. Each and every day we can show random acts of kindness.

If we are going to make this world better, it starts with us. Have you ever experienced a complete stranger walking over to you and placing money in your hand at the unction of the Holy Spirit? Perhaps a person standing in line behind you at the check-out has said, "I'm paying for that," or for services rendered the provider said "no charge." These "just because" blessings can be both naturally rewarding and spiritually enriching. They can uplift our hearts and renew our hope in humanity. The element of surprise so sweetly demonstrates God's care and delight in blessing His children. The pure love expressed in those "just because" blessings melt my heart every time.

But the real joy for me comes in witnessing the heartfelt expressions of thanks that someone cares or their tears that say, "God, you care about me." I remember surprising a church member with a floral centerpiece that I had arranged one Sunday. She broke into tears saying, "I had just said to God, why can't someone just do something for me sometimes." You see, she was always doing for others. It was my delight to do this for her, but I had no idea what she had prayed. So, take the challenge to touch someone's life each day with an act of kindness, a "just because" blessing for the sheer joy of knowing you have shown God's love.

Prayer Hands

Have any of you ever experienced a throbbing toothache? Or maybe you've had some major dental work done and when the "happy gas" wore off you knew the "real feel" of the pain from the procedure. That kind of pain can be excruciating. The tooth is a small member in our body, much like the tongue, but the pain it can cause in given circumstances can bring you to tears. I don't mean to bring back unpleasant memories, but there just might be a noteworthy thought here. A "real" toothache, especially when unchecked, can possibly lead to infection, facial swelling or other aches in the body.

On one of my many dental visits, I was driving home after having a root canal procedure. Well, that "real feel" pain started to kick in, and I wasn't sure that I could continue driving. With one hand on the side of my face and the other on the steering wheel, I went on. The pain could be seen and felt on my face. In passing by a church member's apartment near my home, I decided to stop for prayer. Yes, prayer. I went in and did not have to explain much. She laid her hands on my face and began to pray and speak God's Word for healing and relief from the pain. She prayed for a short time. But I tell you, when she removed her hands from my face, the pain was gone. I do mean literally gone. Praise God!

Hallelujah! I know for myself that God answers prayer. There may be a time that you have to lay hands on and pray for someone or lay hands on yourself and pray. But do it! Use those prayer hands in faith and watch God's Word Work!

Can I Get A Witness

During a Sunday Morning Service in August 2016, the minister began the message with a demonstration on the principle of sowing and reaping, the giving of tithes and offerings with the promised blessings and benefits therewith. Scripture references were given from both the old and new testaments of the Bible that supported these principles. For me, the greatest reference given was that of our Heavenly Father who loved us so much that He gave His only begotten Son, Jesus, the First as the (seed) for our redemption that there might be many sons (harvest), the greatest offering that we might receive the promised benefits. A better understanding of these principles requires one to give due diligence to study.

But let me get back to what happened during the service. At a point in the demonstration, the congregation was asked if there was a mother in attendance that was without a job. After a few moments, someone raised their hand. She slowly and somewhat reluctantly made her way to the front. She was invited to the platform and assured that there was no intent to embarrass her. Standing on the platform, she was handed an envelope with five $5 bills and then asked if she was willing to give one of the $5 bills back. She did. She was then handed another envelope with more bills and was asked if she was willing to give one of those bills back. Yet again, she did. She was handed another envelope with more bills. This time, she did not wait to be asked to give one of the bills back. It seemed that she had now begun to understand the principle of tithing and the benefits therewith. But wait. She was handed yet another envelope. Overcome with joy and grateful emotion, she fell to her knees. You can imagine that the congregation erupted with praise and glory to God. Many were stirred by the Spirit of God, the Spirit of Love, and began bringing more money to the altar. When the mother finally regained her composure, she was assisted to her feet and immediately gave the bill from the envelope. Listen, that's not all. She was now given another envelope and went forth in a praise dance giving the bill while praising God.

The congregation joined in praise and dance all the while bringing more money to the altar. The monies were gathered and given to this mother without a job. You should know, it was a while before the minister was able to continue the message. But truthfully, the message had already been preached. The mother committed that Sunday to prove God in giving tithes and offerings. What a mighty move of the Spirit of God in the demonstration of His Word. *Bring ye all the tithes into the storehouse...* as we are admonished in Malachi 3:10.

Honor And Order

The God of all wisdom and power created the world and all therein. All was finished, it was good and in order as so ordained by the God of Order. Instructions were given and rules were set. Man was given the right of choice to follow God's order. Simply stated, he had a free will to obey or disobey. We know the story of Adam and Eve's choice as written in Genesis and the consequences of their disobedience as realized throughout time for all mankind. Yes, we live in a society where rules are given, boundaries are set and laws are made for a reason. Without them, we would find ourselves in a state of utter chaos and ruin—every man living according to his conscious. We need only read the many accounts in the scriptures or consider the state of affairs in our world today.

We understand God's desire for communion and fellowship with His creation—Man. He created Man after His likeness and communed with him in the Garden of Eden. God brought forth and presented to Adam the gift of woman as a helpmate and companion that they could know, understand and experience communion and relationship spiritually and naturally. God established the family and gave structure for the sacredness of His order. The order of family was not just for "in the beginning", even though the present social climate reflects otherwise. God's Word is the truth anyhow. He spoke in Matthew 24:35, *Heaven and earth shall pass away, but my words shall not pass away.* In Isaiah 40:8 we read, *The grass withereth, the flower fadeth: but the word of our God shall stand forever.* Consider the words of Psalm 119:160, *Thy word is true from the beginning: and every one of Thy righteous judgments endureth forever.* We are inundated with views that lead us to believe that if we "so choose to forgo" the perfect order of God, we may so do and it's the accepted norm in today's world. Many convince themselves that God's standard has changed and that if others are not on board with this way of thinking, then they are out-of-touch with the reality of the present and old fashioned. Let me tell you, it is written in Malachi 3:6, *For I am the Lord, I change not...*

We need only observe family structure today or lack thereof to understand how far society has strayed from God's order. Many hearts have been so seared from the law of God that the world accepts the lower base nature of mankind as the norm. When a people deviate from God's set structure, there's a price to be paid. *For the wages of sin is death...* as we are warned in Romans 6:23. A dear and wise friend of mine summed up her view of the current state of affairs relative to family in saying, "When the man is out of place, the woman is displaced and the children are misplaced." I tend to believe her statement to be an accurate assessment of what we observe today.

The passions of life can be enticingly bittersweet. We do make mistakes. Sometimes, we may know the truth and willingly succumb to our flesh. Granted, it happens, but we don't have to stay there or continue therein. God's love covers a multitude of sins as we repent, ask and allow God to strengthen us in those areas of our weaknesses. His Grace and mercy is availed to us as we look to Him.

The world was created and established with order and structure as so designed by the Almighty God. As God's creation, we demonstrate our love for Him when we Honor His Word, His Precepts, His Principles, His Order, His Structure. Jesus asked Peter the question in John 21, *Lovest thou me?* Upon his response, Jesus gave him a charge to keep. The question remains today, Do you love The Lord? His charge today to each of us is given in John 14:15. It reads, *If ye love me, keep my commandments.*

Relevant Word

Most of us have probably experienced the dreaded paper sort. No matter how many times we put it off, there comes a day when we must go through the tedious process of sorting, discarding or deleting; otherwise, we might find ourselves overwhelmed with paper or electronic messages whether connected to work, home, phone or other electronic devices. Paper sorting extends to emails, texts, mailings, filings or whatever demands our reading.

The day had come and my mind was set to open those paper-stuffed file drawers, folder-filled cabinets and commence with the paper purge. The theme music from jaws rang in my ears, but I was determined, "Those papers were going down." While looking through the papers I realized that many of them were "no longer relevant" and should have been discarded long before this. Time had passed, things had changed, and some papers were outdated. When the task was finished, trash bags were filled with "no longer relevant" papers. It was liberating to rid myself of that which was no longer useful, and it gave a more spacious look to the file drawers and cabinet shelves. And, yes, it gave me that "feel good" sense of accomplishment. The process was tedious, time consuming, but necessary and personally rewarding when done.

Some while later, my thoughts went back to those discarded papers. I pondered how during the course of time some might consider the written Word of God as "no longer relevant." In their conscious mind and practice they discard or disregard those parts of the scriptures deemed by them to be outdated. We are given charge in 2 Timothy 2:15 to *Study to shew thyself approved unto God, a workman that needeth not to be ashamed, rightly dividing the word of truth.* In doing so, John 16:13 tells us, *Howbeit when He, the Spirit of Truth, is come, He will guide you into all truth: for He shall not speak of Himself; but whatsoever He shall hear, that shall He speak...* As Christians or otherwise, we are not given liberty to ignore or discard at will that which does not suit our fancy or that we deem not relevant for the present day mindset or political climate. God's Word is from everlasting to everlasting. 2 Timothy 3:16 tells us that *All scripture is given by inspiration of God, and is profitable for doctrine, for reproof, for correction, for instruction in righteousness...* Moreover, Revelation 22:19 warns that *And if any man shall take away from the words of the book of this prophecy, God shall take away his part out of the book of life, and out of the holy city, and from the things which are written in this book.* The Lord tells us in Matthew 24:35 that *Heaven and earth shall pass away, but my words shall not pass away.* He also says in Malachi 3:6 *For I am the Lord, I change not...* The Word of God is relevant for yesterday, today and all tomorrows.

Raising In The Praising

In times of adversity, there seems to be a natural tendency to fret or complain about the situation. I propose to you that those are just the times to lift your hands in praise to God rendering Him as Lord of All. Magnify Him and not the situation. Mind you, I'm not saying this is in any way easy when you're right in the middle of what may be a crisis situation, but it is the way because He is the way. He is the way of comfort, of strength, of guidance, of forgiveness, of love. We can rest assured of God's presence. We can declare in agreement with His Word as recorded in Romans 8:28, *And we know that all things work together for good to them that love God, to them who are the called according to his purpose.* Whether we realize the good at that present moment or not, trust the Word of God. Look beyond that present moment and praise God for His answer to our need, no matter how great or small.

I've always found my Father God to be faithful. It's an awesome experience for me each time God reveals Himself in my life. He is so much in the details. I'm reminded of a time where I returned to my vehicle after a downtown concert to find it on a flat tire.

And, no, I didn't have the "know how" to change it. It was late at night and everyone was leaving the concert, but no one passing by offered assistance. I made my need known unto God and just thanked Him for the answer. He brought to my mind a church member that could be working late at our local church that was about five minutes away from the downtown area. It was after 9 p.m. I made the call and you know he answered. He was at the church alone, but was finishing up his work. He came immediately, unlatched my spare from underneath the vehicle, changed it out and put things in place. He had me ready to go in a short time, and I'll always remember and appreciate his willingness to avail himself as a Good Samaritan in answer to prayer.

I just do believe when we praise God and begin to thank Him for the answers to our needs, *He hastens His Word to perform it* in our lives as referenced in Jeremiah 1:12. There is a "Raising in the Praising." As we praise God through it all, we realize a lifting in our spirit that brings our heart to a deeper love and gratefulness for His presence, His love, His care.

Reason For Praise

When life seems to have dealt you a bad hand, what do you do? No offense intended for those non-playing card people out there. Just what are we to do when bad things happen in life? It doesn't matter whether they happen to the good or the bad, Christian or not. As God's Children, we look to the author and finisher of our faith. We look to the only wise God who knows the end from the beginning. He knows who we are, where we are and how we are. He knows our frame and we must not think Him to blame for the troubles of life. He assures us in Jeremiah 29:11, *For I know the thoughts that I think toward you, saith the Lord, thoughts of peace, and not of evil, to give you an expected end.*

The story of Job gives understanding and testimony of one that experienced trouble. He was a righteous man that lost his family—except for his wife; his wealth and his health. He sat in sackcloth and ashes listening to three friends' judgment and assessment of his plight. Job even regretted the day he was born. Nevertheless, when all was said and done, Job repented and acknowledged God as sovereign over all. *Then Job answered the Lord, and said, I know that thou canst do every thing and that no thought can be witholden from thee. Who is he that hideth counsel without knowledge? Therefore have I uttered that I understood not; things too wonderful for me, which I knew not* as recorded in Job 42:1-3. This Chapter concludes in verse 12-13, *So the Lord blessed the latter end of Job more than his beginning: for he had fourteen thousand sheep, and six thousand camels, and a thousand yoke of oxen, and a thousand she asses. He had also seven sons and three daughters.*

No, we don't always understand the who, what or why of things, but our trust, faith, and hope should always be in the Father God. Do not magnify the situation, but magnify the Lord. Praise and exalt Him even in those most difficult times. There is a raising in the praising. You hesitate. Have you ever tried it? God says to us in Isaiah 26:3, *Thou wilt keep him in perfect peace, whose mind is stayed on thee: because he trusteth in thee.* We are also encouraged in Philippians 4:8, *Finally, brethren, whatsoever things are true, whatsoever things are honest, whatsoever things are just, whatsoever things are pure, whatsoever things are lovely, whatsoever things are of a good report; if there be any virtue, and if there be any praise, think on these things.* What is it in your situation that you can thank God for. Oh yes, there is something.

Should it be the loss of a loved one, then you can thank the Father God for the time He gifted you with their presence in your life. You can receive the comfort that only He can give and allow Him to heal the hurt. Should it be a job lay-off, then you can thank God for the knowledge, skills and experience garnered while there as a part of your work experience and for the opportunities that are now before you as He leads you to your next job assignment. He is our provider, you know. Perhaps it may be a health issue. We can thank God that this too shall pass and for the testimony of His healing. Thank God for health care professionals and caregivers that He has skilled and provided during the time of illness. Know for a surety that God is the Great Physician. He is the Giver and Sustainer of all life.

Whatever the situation, you can thank God for His abiding love. Trust Him in the process of it all. You are encouraged to read Psalm 34. Verse 1 of that chapter reads, *I will bless the Lord at all times: His praise shall continually be in my mouth.* Verse 3-4 continues, *O magnify the Lord with me, and let us exalt His name together. I sought the Lord, and He heard me, and delivered me from all my fears.* We are reminded here that Psalm 34:19 tells us *Many are the afflictions of the righteous: but the Lord delivereth him out of them all.* Right in the midst of all our troubles, we always have reason to praise God.

No Goodbyes,
Just See You Later

Even in the mother's womb, we become attached.
When born we continue our attachment as we depend on our parents for food, care and nurture. As set forth by God, we observe this to be so in all of creation. Baby birds chirp for food that its mother brings. Joeys, baby kangaroos, stay in their mothers' pouch for a number of months while being fed and protected. A mother hen broods over her baby chicks and provides food, protection and warmth, and will crow up against threatening predators while calling her chicks under the protection of her wings. We attach to others through natural relationships or those that we develop over time. Sometimes, relationships may deepen, be strained, severed or evolve into what may be termed as "complicated." Whatever the case, we are yet dependent or attached to something or someone whether for the good or bad.

For those earthly relationships that nurture and support our well-being through love and care, it is natural to respond and reciprocate love. These relationships may develop into strong soul ties through the bond of family as established by God. Across the years, the bonds of love and family grow deeper, and our hearts are made glad by the gift of their presence in our lives. We are thankful for the season and the time that they are gifted to us. In Ecclesiastes 3:1-2 we read, *To everything there is a season, and a time to every purpose under heaven: A time to be born, and a time to die; a time to plant, and a time to pluck up that which is planted...* Yes, we rejoice at the birth, coo at the growth, applaud at the first steps, encourage through years of ups and downs, shed tears in both joy and pain, take pride in strides made or feel sadness and sorrow in saying goodbyes. I reflect here on that season of earthly transition to that eternal place.

As Believers of the Faith in Jesus Christ, we have the promise of knowing there's no need for the sorrow of final goodbyes. We just say, "see you later" as we look towards the day of our meeting and greeting in the place that our Lord and Savior has prepared for them that love Him, that place so fair and sweet. We take heart in that, "see you later" as we rejoice in knowing that attachments last forever when we are connected to the Great I am.

Applause Deserved

If there's anyone to be applauded, my vote would be for teachers who dedicate themselves to the care and nature of our children. They are charged and entrusted with the task of positively impacting the lives of our children during much of their formative years. Standing, looking through the windows into the classroom does not give any real understanding of the tremendous responsibility of teachers.

After serving several limited service appointments at various schools, I became more keenly aware of the many services teachers provide, and I developed a greater sense of respect and appreciation for them. On any given day, they may have to take on the role of nurse, consoler, caregiver, protector, defender, encourager, mentor, mediator, counselor, preacher/teacher, educator and all else that goes with the position. Teaching is an area of ministry that requires one to be gifted and dedicated to service. One must have a heart and love for children regardless of the push back and negative behaviors that are often encountered in the classroom. By all means, one has to keep the sake of the children in the forefront of their mind despite administrative obstacles or paperwork overload. Though work schedules are set for this job, countless hours are spent outside of that time planning and praying for those children in the role of teacher. Many days, after having poured out so much of themselves, teachers leave the school exhausted in mind and body. Sometimes it can be a bit discouraging and they might wonder if it's all worth it, but somehow an extra surge of energy comes that compels them to press on.

Without a doubt, teachers have the lives of our children in their hands. They are to impart that which will build them up, that which will inspire and motivate them to give their best and be their best selves as they grow and develop to be young adults in society. Teachers help to lay the foundation for future generations to make positive impacts and contributions to our world.

Let's applaud the teachers. Parents, applaud them by being supportive of their efforts and by following God's instruction to *Train up a child in the way he should go: and when he is old, he will not depart from it,* as instructed in Proverbs 22:6, *And, ye fathers, provoke not your children to wrath: but bring them up in the nurture and admonition of the Lord* as written in Ephesians 6:4, and again in Colossians 3:21, *Fathers, provoke not your children to anger, lest they be discouraged.* We all have a part to do. Let us do it well for the sake of our children and future generations.

Mature Minded

The human brain has been the subject of much study. Try as we might to unlock or discover the secrets that lie within, I'm inclined to agree with the idea that some things are past finding out. When awed by the mind of a child prodigy or people who display what we might term as "super human" skills, no matter the age, we can agree that some things cannot be explained with the natural mind. We must inevitably conclude that God does work in mysterious ways; ways that cannot be explained from observation or study.

Varying pools of thought, however, exist that reference the findings of research and clinical studies relative to the aging brain. While spanning the stations on my TV one Sunday afternoon, a documentary that addressed the aging brain in seniors drew my attention. My ears perked up as I tuned in to the research and clinical findings. Several findings that were presented challenged some prevailing thought on the subject. Let me be clear, it is not the intent here to embark on a study of the human brain, but rather to challenge some views of the aging brain in one particular segment of society—the seniors. As my mom, would say, if you live long enough, you will one day be one. Yes, YOU.

Although society at large has attributed forgetfulness, senility, and the like to seniors, everything is not all black and white. You don't have to be a senior to struggle with instant recall. I can remember using the term "data overload on the brain" when attempting to recollect and relay some bit of information in my young adult years. As it turns out, that term sheds some insight relative to the thought and response process of the aging brain. As seniors, according to that study, we acquire and store a wealth of knowledge in our brains over the course of our lives. When retrieving information, our brain has to filter through a lot more data than the younger sect. So, yes, seniors may take more time to respond when answering. Remember, they are speaking from a wealth of knowledge and wisdom. Give those senior saints a "high five."

Another finding from that study of the aging brain concluded that seniors were more inclined to speak the truth, to be honest and candid in their response. You must admit, seniors have a way of speaking their mind. And if you think about it, we give them senior license to do so, no questions asked. Isn't that refreshing to know that someone is being honest and not have to wonder if they are telling you the truth.

The documentary profiled the lives of some seniors that seem to excel in their creative abilities in their elder years. They exhibited a liberty and freedom to explore avenues of creativity not realized in earlier years. Perhaps seniors enjoy a freedom of expression earned with age that allows them to readily explore the depths of their creative side. They can creatively be themselves without the concerns of what others think.

As I noted the findings of the research study presented in the documentary, hope was renewed in the quality of my Golden Years. It was encouraging to know that findings of recent studies indicated that the normal aging process leaves most mental functions intact, that we do not lose brain cells as we age, and that the aging brain is far more resilient than previously thought.

Let's recap these positive notes on the Mature Mind of our senior population. Seniors require more retrieval time to filter through the massive amount of data stored in their brains during the course of their long life. They are not necessarily slow after all. There's just more data to filter through. Seniors are more inclined to speak the truth, to be honest and candid in their response. Let's be honest, we all know that seniors speak their mind. Seniors are more in tune to the carefree, playful spirit as can be noted in how well they interact with the grands. You know it's true! Seniors seemingly explore creative avenues without the concerns of what others think. Let's give it up for our Mature Minded Seniors.

Mama's Missing

On a mid-summer evening in July, we were all casually going about the day's task around home. My sister and brother-in-law were visiting with me after our family reunion. We were all somewhat worn from all the reunion festivities and glad to have this downtime. My sister was upstairs gathering up some of their things for packing and such, my brother-in-law was in the kitchen having a snack, and my mama was in her bedroom resting—so I thought. I passed by her bedroom door, but she was not there. Called out, no response. Went to the deck and looked there. I asked my brother-in-law if he had seen her pass through while sitting in the kitchen. I made one more thorough search throughout the house, outside and around the house, but mama was nowhere to be found.

All of this was a bit puzzling. The thought of the rapture crossed my mind, but I quickly dismissed it because that couldn't be, I was still here. Mama was missing. So as a last resort, I went upstairs to secure the help of my sister to find her. Yes, you're right—there she was. We all had a big laugh. My sister had also been surprised when she looked up and there mama stood. You see, it had been years since my mama had even attempted to climb those stairs. But this time, she had determined to climb or should I say crawl up the stairs and see what was going on up there. The mystery of, "Mama's Missing" was solved, and a lesson was learned. Commit yourself to reaching your destination even if you have to climb, crawl, and rest a bit. Keep moving and you, no doubt, will make it.

A Liberating Word

I heard many a hail and brimstone sermons growing up in church. It just seemed like all the fun things were a sin. The female gender was really kept in check. No make-up, no wearing pants, dresses not too short, hats on your heads and quiet in church were among the many dos and don'ts. The preacher gave the message with fire and fury, and did it ever cause us children to walk in fear and trembling wanting to stay in God's good graces. The preacher would always read the scripture from Deuteronomy 22:5, *The woman shall not wear that which pertaineth unto a man, neither shall a man put on a woman's garment: for all that do so are abomination unto the Lord thy God.* We often heard him say, if you wore pants as a female you were going to hell. Well, I didn't want to go there!

Once though, my dad had us girls helping to cut down some bushes and briers while clearing some land. We put on some pants so that the briers would not scratch our legs. How clearly I remember a little old lady that lived in a house back of the land we were clearing yelling out in her squeaky voice, "You're going to hell with those pants on." That stayed with me all through my young adult life.

Another time I ventured to dare wear pants or something called skorts when I joined a ladies base-ball team from work. We were slated to play a game one evening. As fate would have it, the church choir had an invitation to sing that same evening and I was a member of the choir, but I elected to play with the team.

As it turned out, the opposing team was short of players and I was drafted to side with them and help make up the number needed to play. This was not good. If I played well, my real team would not like it, and if I played bad, the opponents would think I was trying to sabotage the game. Try as hard as I might, there was just no way to feel good about this situa-tion. I missed catching balls, was put out at bat—and to make matters worse, a team member stomped on my foot while crossing the base I was manning. I left that game with hurt feelings and a throbbing foot. As the evening went on, the throbbing worsened and my foot became swollen. With each throb, I could hear that old lady yelling, "You're going to hell with those pants on." Yes, I had worn those skorts—too much like pants, and now I was paying the price. I managed to wrap the foot up as tight as I could for some relief, hobbled to work the next day with a crutch, and, yes, I quit the team. No more wearing pants or anything similar thereto for me.

Some years past and God brought me to a place of growth in Him that led me to join a ministry where I lived and worked. You see, I had been traveling back and forth on weekends to the home church where I grew up. The Lord had so blessed me there, but I knew He led me in this move. During a Wednesday night service, a Minister of The House spoke. He referenced the same passage in Deuteronomy 5 that had kept me in check, and so ingrained in my spirit not to wear pants. This Minister's message, however, was not as had been preached. His was a liberating message. I left that service, went home and read the entire chapter, and subsequently, the whole book of Deuteronomy.

The Spirit of God gave revelation and life to me that night and freed me from that which had held me in bondage and fear for so many years. When I read those scriptures and pondered the message from that Wednesday night service, I realized that the choice before me was to either live a life of dos and don'ts or live a life under the Grace of God. It was clear. As I begin to pray, I said, "Lord, You have provided a better way for me, and I choose Grace." Thank God for "His Liberating Word."

Override

While having the oil changed in my vehicle, the service extended much beyond the usual wait time. Eventually, I inquired as to why. The service manager could only tell me that the technicians would be getting to it. It had already been nearly two hours and no one had even started on the oil change. Besides that, I had a scheduled appointment service time. I politely made the service personnel aware of my concerns.

In the meantime, a gentleman that I had noticed earlier in the waiting area walked over and greeted me. He had a warm pleasant smile. Having heard part of my conversation with the service manager, he began to share his experience and wait for auto service. As we talked further, the conversation centered on spiritual things. Most interesting to me was the discussion about facts and truth. As we continued, I commented how facts can be presented that we do not deny, but beyond the facts there is the truth. He replied back, "Yes much like an override switch. When something malfunctions and shuts down, we can flip the override switch and it starts up again." A hallelujah praise and excitement welled up in my spirit at that Word. He wasn't a "Minister", but did he ever bless my soul.

I pondered on that and began to reflect on how that thought applied to the Word of God. Truth overrides facts. When there are reports of what's considered, "bad news" no matter the cause, we do acknowledge the facts of the matter, but we don't settle for that. We seek God for His guidance in the situation while we continue to walk in faith the more, and stand steadfast in and on the Word of God. We, as Believers, know that God's Word is truth. Praise God, the truth overrides the facts. About the time that I finished this conversation, a service technician walked up to let me know my vehicle was ready and I was good to go, no charge. And that's the truth.

Perspective and Possibility

As a designer, I am more so focused on the creative aspect of a project. There's an excitement about the creative elements of a project that, for me, sometimes overshadow the how to. Of course, the use, application, appropriateness and other factors that may affect the design must be considered. But, as much as you check and double check, it sometimes happens that something has been overlooked that can cause a problem.

That was the case, as I recall, for a design project which seemed simple enough. Measure, determine type product, style, color, allow for needed cutouts in the wood blinds and install. But on the job site, my installer and I found ourselves pondering how to get around an obstruction that I had not accounted for. Cutouts had been made in the wooden slats for the obstruction, but I had not considered the headrail. No cutting through that! We completed the other part of the installation while thinking about and—yes, praying for direction how to possibly address our little dilemma.

It's here that I remember one of my brothers saying to me, "If you can think it, it can be done." And the scripture does say in Matthew 19:26... *With men this is impossible; but with God all things are possible.* Back to the install. Thank God for divine direction and an installer that has a "how to" perspective of things. God does give us our several abilities. As we considered the task at hand, the installer proposed a re-string up to the cutout point of the wood slats, then to bring the entire blind with the headrail up and over the obstruction, thus clearing and allowing us to mount the blind. This would require patience, precision and know-how.

Now, you may not understand or envision the mechanics of the procedure, but let me tell you it worked! Though the install took a lot longer, the look was just what I had designed. The client was quite pleased with the wood blinds, but could not figure out how we did it. As for me and the installer, that was our little secret. When God gives you a vision for something, it's possible!

The "I Can Spirit"

A home will undoubtedly require upkeep, and as homeowners we understand home maintenance to be part of our due diligence. It was no different for me. So, while some contractors were working at a neighbor's home, I inquired about the cost for one of my many home repair projects. The quote was more than I expected or wanted to pay for the project. As much as I needed and wanted the work done, it seemed that this would just have to wait a while longer. But I just kept thinking about the project. I began to ponder and pray about the work. As I did so, I felt the Spirit of God speak to my heart and say, "You Can Do That." I responded, "Okay." My thoughts went immediately to the scripture in Philippians 4:13, *I can do all things through Christ which strengtheneth me.*

Now, my research began for the "how to" DIY project. This was something beyond the scope of work I had ever done before. Nevertheless, after gathering the needed information and materials, I commenced work with the resolve, "I Can Do It." The project took longer than expected but each step of the journey brought me a greater sense of accomplishment and joy in knowing that God was the Master Carpenter and Designer in all of this.

Once completed, friends and family came by. They were amazed at the finished work even commenting that it looked as if it had come right out of a magazine. You can imagine how surprised they were when I told them that I had done the work. I could only tell them that when God says, "You Can Do That", then put on your "I Can" hat and get started.

Appreciate Your Gifting

At a quiet moment during the early morning hours, my thoughts centered on the nature of God's creation to follow and flow in simple and unquestionable obedience to the purpose for which it was created. In the scope of God's plan of creation—He spoke, He commanded, and it was. The birds fly and sing praises unto Him. The sea stays its bounds in humbleness to His command. The fish swim in the seas and oceans deep, not to veer from it of their own accord. The trees burst forth in the spring with green in applause of new life. The soil brings forth its harvest yield as so set by God's times and seasons. The moon glows and reveals itself at the appointed time. The stars twinkle in the backdrop of the night's sky as God flung them in their place. The sun shines without fail at God's setting. The clouds let down their rain for the watering of the earth at God's provision. All creatures, great and small, follow God's bidding in its gifting. A lesson we could all learn and heed just by considering nature's response of obedience to God's will and plan. What a lovely thought, what a lovely picture to behold.

What's God plan and will for your life? Are you walking in humble obedience to His purpose for you? It's in that place of gifting that you realize His blessings and find fulfillment. It's there that you experience great joy and peace. It's there that you please God and you know the grace of His favor. God's love is showered upon all. He has a plan and a purpose for each of us. Pray for clarity in knowing your gifts or gifting. Function therein, and know that it was especially designed with you in mind.

Know from Romans 11:29 that... *the gifts and calling of God are without repentance.* Remember what God says about you in the words of Jeremiah 29:11, *For I know the thoughts that I think toward you, saith the Lord, thoughts of peace, and not of evil, to give you an expected end.* Be mindful of Psalm 139:14, 17, *I will praise thee; for I am fearfully and wonderfully made: marvelous are thy works; and that my soul knoweth right well; How precious also are thy thoughts unto me, O God! how great is the sum of them!* Appreciate the wonderful gift God has granted you and look not to another. Praise God for the opportunity to just be and be part of the Master's Plan.

God's Way

When God gives us something to do, we are to know that He has equipped and empowered us to do it. We are not to lean to our own understanding, but acknowledge Him and let Him lead the way. He is the way, the truth and the light. Move "self" out of the way and let God's Spirit have free course. All we need to do is believe, walk in faith and trust Him every step of the way. That's what the patriarchs of old did.

When Abram was instructed to leave his people and his home and go to the place that God would lead him—he did, not knowing where but trusting God. After receiving the promised son, Isaac, Abraham made the faith journey as required by God to offer his son as a sacrifice unto God—not asking why. He believed God would provide Himself a lamb for the sacrificial offering when questioned and God did just that for there was a ram in the bush.

Moses, during the forty year journey leading the Children of Israel out of Egypt, believed God, though threatened by Pharaoh and his army, and dealing with the murmurings and the rebellion of the people. Moses could not journey in his own sufficiency; He had to trust God to be the way—all the way, as he walked in obedience. We understand from this account written in the Book of Exodus that God made a highway through the Red Sea for the people to cross and for them to see their adversaries no more. God brought forth water gushing out of a rock, He rained down breakfast, lunch and dinner form heaven to sustain them, He led them with a cloud by day and a pillar of fire by night. Talk about being the Way and leading the Way—God did that and so much more.

Now David has his own account of God's leading as well. David did not look to his own stature when facing the lion or the bear as a little shepherd boy, but believed God for the victory. Likewise, when facing Goliath, he did not look to other's amour, weaponry or stature, but trusted God to be his way of victory in proclaiming before Goliath in 1 Samuel 17:45 *Thou comest to me with a sword, and with a spear, and with a shield: but I come to thee in the name of the Lord of hosts...* We know from 2 Corinthians 10:4 that... *the weapons of our warfare are not carnal, but mighty through God to the pulling down of strong holds...* Yes, David took those three small stones in his hand and it took only one "God directed" stone to bring victory.

New Testament scriptures give account of the many miracles that Jesus did and His disciples. Notice, I did say, and His disciples. Remember, it was Peter who walked on the water as long as he looked to Jesus—The Way. Only when he observed the winds and waves did he began to sink. Nevertheless, Jesus was right there to save. Again the lesson to note here is "Keep Your Eyes on The Way."

Holy Obedience

Has Holy fear ever struck you when the Spirit of God spoke to your heart to move forward with a certain task or mission? You may have sat or stood wondering who am I to do this or felt like you weren't qualified. We read in the scriptures of those like Moses who encountered God in the burning bush and was commission to be the spokesperson to lead God's people out of Egypt into the Promised Land. He too responded likewise—questioning his qualifications.

While sitting in a Sunday night church service some years back, I felt the spirit of God prompting me to speak out that the men of the ministry were to surround our Pastor and pray, but I stood frozen and hesitant about doing such a thing. Who was I as a young woman in the congregation to step forward when there were so many seasoned saints among us? Surely they could hear the voice of God. I couldn't bring myself to move out. It was then another brother went up on the platform and spoke the thing that God had given me. I felt so ashamed and repentant of not obeying the voice of God. I began to pray and ask for God's forgiveness. As I watched the men lay hands on and strengthen our Pastor in prayer, the Spirit of

God again spoke to me that the women were to go forth and anoint our Pastor with oil. You can believe I could hardly wait until the men finished praying. The thought of not being obedient to the voice of God and feeling of disappointment made me more fearful of standing still. I wasted no time in stepping out and speaking what God had spoken after the men prayed. They had prayed, but not anointed. The women did just what God had spoken.

God was and is gracious to us when we may feel weak, afraid or unworthy of the task set before us. He knows our frame and His strength is made perfect in our weakness. In Isaiah 6, we find Isaiah saying as he envisioned the Holy and Glorious Lord, *Then said I, Woe is me! for I am undone; because I am a man of unclean lips, and I dwell in the midst of a people of unclean lips: for mine eyes have seen the King, the Lord of hosts. Then flew one of the seraphim unto me, having a live coal in his hand, which he had taken with the tongs from off the altar: And he laid it upon my mouth, and said, Lo, this hath touched thy lips; and thine iniquity is taken away, and thy sin purged. Also I heard the voice of the Lord, saying, Whom shall I send, and who will go for us? Then said I, Here am I; send me.* I've heard said, "Whom God calls, He qualifies." We need only be obedient to His call.

Something Out of Nothing

Within family, we all know the blessing of a mother's love and tender care when we reflect on those fond thoughts and memories. My family always had lots of gatherings celebrating birthdays, holidays and special occasions. But it didn't have to be a special occasion. We came together as family to work around the home or just fellowship. Most times our gatherings were planned. At other times, we showed up impromptu when mama hadn't pre-planned or wasn't expecting all of us. One thing was constant though. Mama would make sure there was food spread on the table. She would go in the kitchen, start pulling things out of the pantry cabinets, refrigerator, freezer, and before we knew it she would be ringing a little dinner bell mounted to the kitchen wall letting us know the meal was ready.

A nephew once commented, "Grandmamma can make something out of nothing." That's the truth, the whole truth and nothing but the truth. Mama relayed to us her childhood memories of doing chores on the farm, in the fields, and in the house through which she learned the value of hard work. She told us about walking to the little country school each day to learn and receive an education. I remember her telling us stories about how they worked with what God provided and never wanted or lacked. Many a times I've heard my mama recite Psalm 37:25, *I have been young, and now am old; yet have I not seen the righteous forsaken, nor his seed begging bread.*

I recall some of my own testimonies of this truth. During a season in my life I experienced a financial stretch like none other. Those times when your gas hand is ever pointing to "excitement," little or no food in the cabinets or refrigerator, you don't turn on the AC, but sweat it out in the heat to save on utilities and the like. Life happens, but we must yet trust God. It was such a situation in my life that I found myself hungry and wondering what, if anything, was there to eat. I found a box of macaroni, but no cheese pack. Then, I spied a package of leftover seasoning mix from a bag of popcorn. I proceeded to prepare my evening meal. When the dish was finished, I had the best tasting Green Onion Macaroni Casserole ever. Let me tell you that whatever has been given to your hands, God can direct you how to make something out of that which seems to be nothing. Inquire of God's Will and Direction in your situation. Believe! Praise Him! It's in the house! Seek and you will find! Knock and the door will be opened unto you! Ask and it shall be given unto you!

Request for Cotton

Can you solve this riddle? What is brown and woody, yet white, light and fluffy all over? Did you guess it? Yes, it's cotton. For those who don't know what that is, it's the fluffy white stuff that's grown on a stalky plant and used to make some of the clothing that you and I wear, bed linens and other fabric items. Let me ask you another question? Have you ever seen those stalks of white fluffy cotton bolls grown in late December? There they were. Stalks and stalks of them right upstairs in the Family Room of my home. I'm sure you are intrigued by all of this. So, let me explain.

I inquired, prayed and asked God to help me locate and acquire stalks of cotton to complete a design project that had been in the making for over a year. You see, this crop is regionally and seasonably grown in the fall and should be harvested during that time; otherwise, it may be another year before it's possibly available. There were those that I had asked to help me locate and find this item, but to no avail. Nevertheless, it was still my desire to find the cotton. The unique and specific request was for cotton stalks. Let me tell you, when the Word of God invites us to make our request known—be specific. That's what I did and God indeed answered me just so. Philippians 4:6 does instruct us to *Be careful for nothing; but in everything by prayer and supplication with thanksgiving let your requests be made known to God.* Furthermore, don't even think about limiting The God of all Creation, *For with God nothing shall be impossible* as referenced in Luke 1:37. When you keep walking in faith with a spirit of expectancy, God will show Himself strong on your behalf. How did God do this for me? I'm glad you asked.

While ushering for a stage theatre production, it just so happened that the set was staged with stalks and stalks of cotton. Yes, cotton. There it was. It was just what I had prayed and asked for. I inquired—and when the run of the production was done I went right over and was invited to get as much as I wanted. My God had not only answered my request for cotton, but it was abundantly provided, pulled up and brought for me to see and receive. What an awesome God we serve! My spirit leaps within me when I think on His amazing love. I love Him so because He loves me so!

The Hattiesburg Connection

In this life, we quest for love, the need to love and to be loved. It's the dream of most. We as Believers know God's love for us and our love and worship for Him. What a joy it is to receive and know His love. We also desire natural companionship as God ordained it to be so.

While seeking God's guidance in this regard, I met with a group at one of our church member's home for a time of prayer. We all had needs, questions and desires before God and just wanted His direction. As we prayed, the spirit of the Lord began to stir our hearts. We felt His love as joy flooded our souls. The spirit of prophecy came forth and Prophetic Words were given as the Spirit of God moved in our midst through an elder who had been invited as a guest minister. He was older, gentile and small in stature, but you could feel the love and power of God flow through him as He ministered through the gift of prophecy.

With much anticipation, I continued to pray that God would speak through him to me concerning my questions and desires. And God did just that. How well I remember the Prophetic Words that were spoken to me. They were specific and detailed. He said that he saw in the Spirit someone coming into my life. They would be coming from Hattiesburg, MS and they would be driving a new car. Excitement flooded my being while thanksgiving and praise to God filled my heart. Well, you know I began to look and wait for the manifestation of that Prophetic Word.

It was not long that the prophecy began to be revealed just as it was spoken. God is great and His Word is true. I know this for myself. Someone did come into my life, they did come from Hattiesburg, MS and they were driving a new car. All was as had been spoken. However, it was not as I supposed. You see, God had sent the sister of a high school classmate from my hometown to lodge with me for a season while she began a new job. She had just finished school in Hattiesburg, MS and was driving a new car she had bought for work. Smiles all around. God does answer prayer. He blessed me with the best roommate ever who became as a sister to me. She has continued to be a blessing in my life over the years. God is good like that. Get connected and let Him make connections for you.

Matter of Principle

If you don't stand up for right, you're subject to fall for anything, is a slogan that I've heard said and prefaced in conversation myself. Sometimes we may see or experience injustices and have the choice of speaking up or giving silent consent. I recall watching the TV program, "What would you do?" The program highlights staged scenes that gauge the reactions or inaction of people to what might involve controversial issues and could evoke strong feelings. I have found myself tear up or become incensed with the feeling of anger just in watching the staged scenes. In real life, I have also found myself taking up for others that are mistreated and definitely standing up for myself unless the Spirit of God directs otherwise.

So vividly I remember a situation that required a court action to bring justice. A friend had borrowed an item of clothing for a special occasion. She decided to have it cleaned before returning it, but the cleaners had ruined the white laced garment when placing it with some red colored items. You can imagine the red dye on the white garment. My friend called me and apologized for what had happened. Of course, I knew it wasn't her fault. The cleaners refused to reasonably compensate me for the ruined garment. This was not right, and I felt as a matter of principle that it was necessary to follow procedure for initiating a small claim in court.

There's a bit of lawyering in me, so I had prepared with due documentation. After arriving to court, I noted three representatives from the cleaners, but that did not intimidate me at all. When called up, I addressed the judge and explained the situation. He questioned the cleaners. They did not deny ruining the garment, but disputed my requested compensation amount citing garment depreciation as the basis for the offer that had been made. The judge noted the amount offered and my documentation for the amount requested. He also noted that I was well-prepared and commented that what the cleaners had offered was not a sufficient amount to compensate me for the ruined garment. The judge ruled in my favor and instructed the cleaners to, "Pay the woman." I left that day knowing that when you stand up for principles, God will reward. While the Book of Proverbs is devoted to moral values and wisdom for daily living, God instructs us in His laws and principles all throughout the scriptures.

Home Free, No Fear

The experience of moving from an apartment into my first home was exciting and almost hassles free. It was planned and done with such ease, except for packing boxes. As it is with many of us when we move, we wonder where all the stuff came from when we start the task. The Lord blessed me with a small army of friends that offered and almost insisted on helping with the move. They cleaned and prepared the new home, transported all the boxes, furnishings and stuff, put everything in place and celebrated this blessing with me. By the end of move-in day, it looked like I had been living there for years. All the boxes had been unpacked. Pictures were hung on the wall. Rugs carefully placed on the floor. Some family members spent a few days there with me as we enjoyed the home.

The joy of home ownership, however, was almost overshadowed when fear seemed to grip my thoughts. It was like every little creak and sound in the house was magnified. The idea of being alone in a new place, unfamiliar surroundings, and an environment where there were no people on the other side of the wall was a bit scary. My nights became more and more restless.

How could the joy of my blessing become a torment to me? God had given me this home and it was blessed. I prayed and asked Good for His Peace.

I looked forward to Sunday Church Services. The thought of being in fellowship with other Christians as we worshiped, praised, and received the Word of God was comforting. The service brought calm and a peace to my heart. Let me tell you, we serve a loving, caring Father that surely hears and answers prayer. The Pastor ministered a message on fear. He talked directly to me. Oh, yes, He did. He expounded on the tactics that the adversary uses to instill fear, and that it was not of God. He referenced 2 Timothy 1:7, *For God hath not given us the spirit of fear; but of power, and of love, and of a sound mind.* That Sunday, I experienced the scripture written in John 8:32, *And ye shall know the truth, and the truth shall make you free.* From that day forward, I slept in peace in my home. I thanked God and praised Him the more that He knows all. He heard my prayers and had answered me speedily.

While we are to exercise due diligence in natural things, we understand and know that only what we entrust to God is secure. Psalm 127:1 says *Except the Lord build the house, they labor in vain that build it: except the Lord keep the city, the watchman waketh but in vain. It is vain for you to rise up early, to sit up late, to eat the bread of sorrows: for so He giveth his beloved sleep.* That home is still a part of me today, and I thank God for the blessing it has been to me and so many others. It's a home of peace and joy, "no fear."

The Plan

World systems bombard our lives daily with offers for plans to protect or secure our persons and property from the dangers, disasters, and devastations that occur in life. Sometimes, they might go so far as to use fear tactics to persuade us of the urgent need to acquire their services. While there may be value in their product, we cannot be guaranteed of total safety. While we are to be diligent when it comes to safety, there is no substitute for God's Protection Plan. Its benefits are boldly printed in His word and you don't have to be concerned about "the small print" or "exclusions."

To acquire the Plan, you need only to say yes to His salvation plan. The Protection Plan is all a part of the package when you receive Jesus as Lord and Savior of your life. God's Protection Plan stipulates in Psalm 4:8, *I will both lay me down in peace, and sleep: for Thou, Lord, only makest me dwell in safety;* Psalm 121:5-8 *The Lord is thy keeper: the Lord is thy shade upon thy right hand. The sun shall not smite thee by day, nor the moon by night. The Lord shall preserve thee from all evil: He shall preserve thy soul. The Lord shall preserve thy going out and thy coming in from this time forth, and even for evermore;* Psalm 40:4, *Blessed is that man that maketh the Lord his trust...;* and Psalm 91, *He that dwelleth in the secret place of the most High shall abide under the shadow of the Almighty. I will say of the Lord, He is my refuge and my fortress: my God; in Him will I trust...* These sections only preview what's in the Plan. God's Protection Plan is not just part of an Insurance Plan, but a part of God's Assurance Plan. So when life's events occur, make sure that you have already been covered under God's Protection Plan and by all means, Read, "The Plan."

Good and Perfect Gift

L et patience have her perfect work, that ye may be perfect and entire, wanting nothing, as referenced in James 1:4.

These were the words uttered to my spirit at a time when I had become a bit anxious about moving to another home. My initial thoughts were "What!" It seemed that I had already been waiting forever. Besides, the environment in which I was currently living was not conducive to my functioning in the real world. You see, I'm one of those persons that like order and structure in my world. In no sense of the word was that the case in the present home environment. Costly repairs were underway. Boxes were already packed and literally stacked to the ceiling in several rooms. Closets were empty and walls had been painted. Plumbing work had been done as well as costly foundation repair. Flooring had been replaced. I had been living out of boxes during the whole process with dust from the hammer jack settling on everything and commuting from one bathroom to the next while sinks were repaired in one and bathtub in the other. This was no fun. I know, just minor inconveniences, but I did indeed grow weary and ready for some order in my life.

Nevertheless, I received God's Word and knew that He was doing something wonderful! The Word of God uttered to my spirit was timely and brought refreshing and calmness. Now, just settle myself and let God be God. Yes, God's Word does say in Philippians 4:6-7, *Be careful for nothing; but in everything by prayer and supplication with thanksgiving let your requests be made known unto God. And the peace of God, which passeth all understanding, shall keep your hearts and minds through Christ Jesus.*

The day came when I was out and about doing errands that I saw a stand of brochures advertising homes for sale. Quickly, I grabbed a few and went about my errands. Later, as I looked through the brochures, one home that was for sale by owner piqued my interest. I called the number listed. An appointment was scheduled. I must admit that I did become a bit anxious, but God calmed my spirit to be patient and wait for the set appointment time. In the meantime, I stood in faith.

On the Sunday afternoon of the appointment I remember ringing the doorbell and being warmly greeted. As I stepped inside, I knew this was my new home. This was my "good and perfect gift." Everything about the home fit me. In fact, the items that I had already purchased in anticipation of the move were just the right colors to fit each room. The owners, a lovely couple, welcomed me to sit down while we talked and discussed the financial aspects of the sale. Well, I offered a lower amount than the asking price. After a few moments, the husband spoke an amount between the asking and offered amount. I agreed and now just had to write a check for the earnest money. Would you believe it, I didn't bring a check. So I told the owners that I would leave and be back to finish things.

Indeed I did and the deal was sealed. The Lord had shown me great favor. During the transaction, the wife shared that while I was away, she asked her husband, "What had they done accepting a lower offer and why?" She said her husband responded, "I like her." And, oh, was I glad that he did. I knew it was the Holy Spirit working and God's Word being fulfilled in due season. The home was dedicated and blessed. It was not for me alone, and over the years it has been a safe haven for many—a house of healing, of peace and of love. Forever, I thank and praise God for entrusting to my hands a "good and perfect gift."

Unnecessary Places

Have you ever been in a place of asking yourself, "What does it all mean?" For a brief moment you feel a sense of emptiness even though there is nothing off kilter. Life can sometimes take you to that place. It does not have to be that you are overwhelmed or underwhelmed with anything, but temporarily lack a realization of purpose and feel so unnecessary; or perhaps, it's a place of self-reflection, and you don't find yourself at that place in life where your heart longs to be. It may be that you have experienced a view of the mountain top and now you are on the downside, alone in the valley.

In all of this, we need to understand that there are many other mountain top views ahead for us to know the awe and wonder. God's timing of things in our lives will always bring us to the good and perfect gifts in due time and you don't have to see to know that God is ever present during those times that you may feel so unnecessary. Arouse and arise from any place of stupor that you might encounter as you begin to meditate on and follow the instructions of Philippians 4:8, *Finally, brethren, whatsoever things are true, whatsoever things are honest, whatsoever things are just, whatsoever things are pure, whatsoever things are lovely, whatsoever things are of good report; if there be any virtue, and if there be any praise, think on these things.* We are not to be anxious. Apply the words of James 1:4, *But let patience have her perfect work, that ye may be perfect and entire, wanting nothing.* Be assured that God's love abounds to us, His heart and thoughts are towards us, and His hand is for us.

All throughout scripture we are told of His ever abiding presence. In Matthew 28:20, He tells us... *lo, I am with you always, even unto the end of the world...* and in Hebrews 13:5, we read... *for He hath said, I will never leave thee, nor forsake thee.* As your spirit begins to be refreshed and renewed, as you begin to sense the excitement and anticipation of where God is leading, whether it be to the next mountain, through the sea, or in a dry place, reflect on God's proven Word. Remember that Moses lead the children of God to safety right through the Red Sea; Abraham took Isaac to the mountain, the place of sacrifice where God provided Himself a lamb; Ezekiel was taken to a valley of dry bones where God commanded him to prophesy unto the bones, and they all were brought together with flesh and breath. They lived and stood as an exceeding great army. Know that we all have a part in God's plan. That's why you are here with your necessary self.

Past Qualifiers

Don't let the past rule your future. There have been reflective moments when I thought about past mistakes, faults, errs, shortcomings or negative experiences. But because of God's grace and mercy there was no need for me to dwell there. When we sin, we repent and receive God's forgiveness. It does not matter whether those faults, failures, or experiences were of our own doing or experienced at the hand of someone else. As victims of negative encounters that were imposed upon us, there may be a tendency to blame ourselves feeling that somehow it was our fault. Know this—God's grace is sufficient. He desires to heal our hurt and our heart as we allow Him to love us, love through us, forgive us, and forgive through us. The past is just that—past. We cannot change what has already happened. We would, however, be wise to remember the past, learn and grow from it so that we don't repeat those past mistakes. Don't stay, get stuck or dwell there. Move forward and let it serve as a reminder of God's keeping and saving grace. God knows our frame and He sees beyond all that we may perceive to be character flaws, shortcomings, faults and failures. Be mindful of God's Word in Philippians 3:13, *Brethren, I count not myself to have apprehended: but this one thing I do, forgetting those things which are behind, and reaching forth unto those things which are before.*

When we read of those heroes of the Scriptures, we just might find they were not perfect in any sense of the Word. Those movers and shakers like Noah, Moses, Abraham, Jacob, David, Solomon, Peter, Paul the Apostle had faults, failures, shortcomings, but were used mightily by God. Yes, God chose them to fulfill some of the greatest missions as recorded in His Word. We need not deem ourselves unworthy or feel that shortcomings disqualify us for service. To the contrary, it may very well be the qualifier for service. The adversary may even try to flood our mind with negative thoughts. But the accuser of the brethren is a liar and the truth is not in him. Don't be ensnared by this tactic. Don't be held captive in your mind from going forth in your gifts and callings.

In the beginning we were as dust. But from the earth God formed man and blew in him the breath of life. He beheld His creation and proclaimed it to be good. Those imperfections that we may see in ourselves or that others are quick to point out serve to bring greater glory to the power of God. It is He that hath made us and not we ourselves. I Samuel 16:7 notes... *for the Lord seeth not as man seeth; for man looketh on the outward appearance, but the Lord looketh on the heart.* What qualifies us as vessels for the Master's use is not the height of our stature nor our countenance, not excellence of speech or perfection of flesh. We yield our broken, imperfect, blemished vessels to The Potter's Hand. He sees and knows the beautiful vessels that we are to be in His hand when others only see globs of clay. That purpose for which He called you to, He qualified you for. The past journey, whether failures or successes, weaknesses or strengths, faults or merits, shortcomings or virtues, imperfections or blemish-free were all in preparation for our calling and mission. We need not dwell or fret over the past. Allow God to teach us thorough those experiences and use them to only bring us to a greater place of service.

Mind Frame

Film production and picture animation involves using a series of still shots or pictures called frames to produce and replicate movement or action. Our eyes, too, serve as receptors or lenses that take still shots or snapshots of what's seen, heard and felt. That then becomes processed and printed from the camera of our minds onto our hearts and produce the frames from which we think, act and do. When we get stuck in a frame, however, problems can arise. When we don't move from a certain mind set, we can become stagnant in that place of thinking. In other words, the complete work that God has gifted us for can be stalled in production, delayed and may never be produced. In scripture, we read of such accounts. Let's consider a few examples.

The Israelites' Journey from Egypt to The Promised Land was stalled. As we understand from the journal of their journey given from Exodus through Joshua, they wandered in the wilderness for 40 years because of unbelief. God had given them a promise, He had given them a series of frames to know His power, yet they were unwilling to believe and go in to possess all that had been given unto them. They were stuck in the frame of unbelief and wandered for 40 years. That's a long time.

In the Book of Jonah we read of his plight. He received a commission from God to go preach repentance to that great city, Nineveh, but chose instead to board a ship elsewhere. He was discovered in that ship of disobedience when a great storm arose on the seas and the others aboard feared for their life. Jonah was tossed overboard to calm the sea only to be swallowed by a great fish. The account goes on to let us know that he stayed in the belly of that fish, in that frame of disobedience, for 3 days and 3 nights before repenting and moving from that frame as the fish spewed him out. He somehow made a 3 day journey in a day. That sounds to me like he ran or maybe even sprinted in obedience towards that city, Nineveh, to preach as God had so commissioned. Don't get stuck in the frame of disobedience. Heed and hearken unto the Word of God. It will save you a lot of headache and heartache.

For all mankind from "in the beginning" God set the framework in motion that we need not stay in the frame of unforgiveness. Woven throughout the thread of scriptures, we read of His Love, His Mercy, His Grace, His Forgiveness towards us. We read in John 3:16, *For God so loved the world, that He gave His only begotten Son, that whosoever believeth in Him should not perish, but have everlasting life.* What amazing love and demonstration of forgiveness. We are taught to forgive others as we have been forgiven. Don't get stuck in the frame of unforgiveness by failing to move beyond past hurts and wounds. Allow God to heal the wounds and move on to the next frame of life so that you can experience the frame of joy and peace, so that you can reap the benefits of God's truth. His Word tells us in Ephesians 4:31-32, *Let all bitterness, and wrath, and anger, and clamour, and evil speaking, be put away from you, with all malice: And be ye kind one to another, tender-hearted, forgiving one another, even as God for Christ's sake hath forgiven you;* Colossians 3:13, *Forbearing one another, and forgiving one another, if any man have a quarrel against any: even as Christ forgave you, so also do ye.;* and Matthew 6:14-15, *For if ye forgive men their trespasses, your heavenly Father will also forgive you: But if ye forgive not men their trespasses, neither will your Father forgive your trespasses.*

Don't let your mind or heart get stuck in the frame of doubt or unbelief, disobedience nor unforgiveness, regret, failures, shame, or blame. Just don't get stuck. No matter the frame, we are to follow after God as we move forward from faith to faith, glory to glory. Allow God to lead and direct the series of frames in your life so that when they are completed you can hear the Director say unto you as in Matthew 25:21... *Well done, thou good and faithful servant...*

Tell It All To God

Don't try to hide from your flesh. It is already revealed in what you do and how you act. Confess your faults, your shortcomings, the areas where you need help. The Father already knows and is patiently waiting for you to invite Him to begin work in your heart and your mind.

I recollect a time when it was difficult for me to walk in love towards someone that hurt me deeply. Wounds were deep, but I didn't like nor did I want to feel that way, so I sought God for the answer. God used someone I had just met to speak to my heart in the midst of a business conversation without me telling them anything about the matter. His Spirit let me know that I could not walk in love towards them on my own, but I could allow Him to love them through me. Praise the Lord! We can always go to the Father for whatever the matter and know that He has the answer. James 5:16 reads, *Confess your faults one to another, and pray one for another, that ye may be healed. The effectual fervent prayer of a righteous man availeth much.*

I wholeheartedly say yes and amen to God's Word. As we confess our faults one to another, we must be mindful to seek God's guidance in whom to confide. Let Him direct your path to those deemed trustworthy and whose lives reflect the love of God, to those who will sincerely pray and speak the Word of God that you may be healed and helped, to those that will not judge, and those that will not "run and tell that." It's unfortunate that sometimes we may find our confidence betrayed, but God will judge that matter. Confess your faults, repent of your sins to God. That's my prevailing thought. As we sincerely repent, God's grace is availed unto us that we receive forgiveness as we forgive others.

Jewels and Gems

O Lord, our Lord, how excellent is thy name in all the earth! These are the words ascribed unto our majestic Lord and King in Psalm 8:9. As I meditate on that thought, I am joyously awakened to some moments that permeate my total being. There are those unforgettable moments that are like rare jewels and gems. When you find them, you cherish your time there and want to hold on to the moments forever. It's the place in time where you breathe in the glorious awe and awareness of God's majesty and presence while basking in the embrace of His gentle love.

Imagine looking out over the vast ocean blue, whose expanse stretches as far as the eye can see and seems to have no end. While there, the cool ocean's breeze softly caresses your face. It's in that moment you know God's power, strength and might in the sweetness of His care. Another time, you stroll down to the pier's end. There you sit taking in that moment of quiet sunshine. The movement of the water lulls you to that place of peace that you never want to leave. You have a panoramic view of snowcapped mountains that almost take your breath away as you behold their peaks that seem to touch the sky. There you stand in wonder of so grand a creation sculpted by the Master's hand. What a moment of sweet surrender to God's glory as you take in a moonlit, starry night. Yet, another moment still at the dawning of the day when the entrance of the sun is announced by radiant beams that shine bright like a diamond. Now the view of earth from eagle's eyes as you look down from space seeing only the crafting of lush green plots bordered by nature's hues and dots of blue. It's a view from which there are no worries.

All cherished moments that take you to a place and time of knowing that you are enveloped in the Father's love. You are assured of safety in the Almighty's strong arm of care. You can rest in the cradle of the Master's peace. You are in the moment of the undeniable presence of the King. But one more moment that surpasses all the others. It's the moment that your mind's eye catches a glimpse of the rugged cross that tells the redemption story. It tells of God's great love that spared not His only son, but looked on you and me and saw a moment.

Spiritual Muscles

Just as a weight lifter spends grueling hours targeting areas and sculpting to train for the sole purpose of developing and refining specific muscles in his body for presentation, you must also spend quality time in the Word and in the War Room to build up your most holy faith and... *present your bodies a living sacrifice, holy, acceptable unto God, which is your reasonable service* stated in Romans 12:1. Time must also be spent in fasting and prayer.

The scriptures record in Mark Chapter 9, the account where the disciples questioned Jesus as to why they were unable to cast out a foul spirit of one deaf and dumb. In verse 29, *And He said unto them, This kind can come forth by nothing, but by prayer and fasting.* You must fortify your spirit with the Word of God; commit His Word to your heart; stand firm on it; apply it to your daily life in worship to the Father; speak it, pray it, let it not depart from you. Modify your diet to include lots of *love, joy, peace, longsuffering, gentleness, goodness, faith, meekness, temperance* as listed in Galatians 5:22. Drink plenty of liquids, being filled with the Holy Spirit. Exercise your faith each and every day as you encounter resistance against truth. Use those encounters to stretch, tone, and sculpt your being into the image of Christ.

The Father will take the heavy out of the weights for He tells us that His Yoke is easy and His burden is light, as referenced in Matthew 11:28-30. He will not put on you any more than you can bear. You may be a bit sore at first, but this too will pass, and you will realize marked results as you go from faith to faith, victory to victory, and glory to glory. Don't wimp out, don't give up, don't quit, but hold fast to the profession of your faith. Keep going and you are guaranteed to be looking good as you stand before the Master Trainer. Now, you need that anointing oil to add that extra glisten and glow. Go ahead, strike that pose, you well-defined, soul-refined Child of the King. Show those Muscles!

Character Recognition

From time to time, I've been pleasantly delighted to enjoy some time of relaxation while watching a Masterpiece Classic. It was just so when I tuned in to some episodes of a PBS broadcast series. The series was not only entertaining but, for me, spiritually enlightening as well. I became intrigued with the roles portrayed by several of the characters—the Queen, the Prince and Lord M. No, this was not a "chick flick", but rather a Masterpiece Classic that shadowed historic events.

Indulge me while I share a bit about my perception of the characters mentioned. Let's begin with Lord M. My spirit recognized him to be the voice of wise counsel always with the presence of command while maintaining a rather quiet demeanor. His responses were always thought provoked, not of flesh to flesh. Though often given invitation to engage in confrontation, he was masterful in recognizing the tactics being employed and was wise to *answer not a fool according to his folly, lest thou also be like unto him, answer not a fool according to his folly, lest he be wise in his own conceit* as we are advised in Proverbs 26:4-5. No, he was not ensnared in needless controversial conversation. He maintained a gentle, calm nature that knew how to politely and graciously excuse himself to peace. While others touted their wealth of knowledge regarding the affairs of state, he responded with only four words. "Knowledge is not Wisdom." Nothing else to be said.

The Queen, of course possessed her own stately character. She grew in grace and wisdom with a love for the people and commitment to the call upon her life. She recognized that her life was not her own. She sought Lord M. for wise counsel and surrounded herself with those who could strengthen her position. That did not mean those who would always agree with her, but those who would tell her the truth. In times of conflicts with herself, she listened to the voice of reason. Does this not remind you of Queen Esther in the scriptures? Now that was and is a "made for movie" Book in the scriptures.

The Prince married into the royal house of the Queen. He possessed his own place as Prince before the union and affirmed his position while respecting and giving due honor to his wife as Queen. Much can be said here of which I give no claim to be qualified to address. Nevertheless, allow me the liberty to give note to some observations. A profession of love was given to the marriage. It was not just one of convenience or political strategy. Love served as the abiding strength to the union during those times of conflict. It's interesting to note here that as we know a man and a woman to be different in person and being, so are their personal internal and external conflicts. The Queen expressed her inner conflict as wife to the Prince. That is as Queen, she must command, but as wife she must submit. Pause, ponder and consider that thought ladies. The Prince experienced his inner conflict as a man who sought to find his place in his new position as husband to the Queen. As a man, he must function in his authority as head, but must also yield and honor the position of his wife as Queen. Give serious thought men to Ephesians 5:25 that reads *Husbands, love your wives, even as Christ also loved the church, and gave himself for it...* Verse 28 continues, *So ought men to love their wives as their own bodies. He that loveth his wife loveth himself.* This sounds like serious business to me.

The Queen and Prince both acknowledged their personal conflicts and were willing to work towards a resolve. In doing so, they both acquired/learned the art of giving due respect and honor to each other's gifting and position while yet continuing in their personal gifting. Recognizing, respecting and yielding to the gift that each possess in marriage might well avert many heartaches and headaches. Would you not agree? I loved watching the scenes where the Queen was always attuned and attentive to support the Prince in his time of personal conflict and the scenes where the Prince was ever present to do likewise for the Queen. But more than that, my heart was made glad when they both united as a powerful force against those external conflicts that do and will present themselves. As Psalm 133:1 advises *Behold, how good and how pleasant it is for brethren to dwell together in unity!* We understand the strength of unity as referenced in Ecclesiastes 4:9-12.

Perhaps, you found yourself in one of the characters mentioned here. In any case, it is my sincere prayer that an encouraging thought has been gleaned; a strengthening Word has been given that resonates within your spirit. I pray that the spiritual fruit recognized in the characters noted here prompts a determination in you to give yourself to wise counsel, to acknowledge your personal inner conflicts and allow the spirit of God to bring you to a resolve. Moreover, I pray that you are provoked to love, to give due honor and respect for the gifts within the body, to work towards the unity of the faith that we dwell together in peace. Amen and Amen.

Temper, Temper

The food network often gives demonstrations of different culinary techniques while preparing mouth-watering dishes. It was interesting to watch the culinary art of tempering that involved mixing a hot dish like soup, stock or a sauce to a cold product like diary or eggs. As I watched the process, a portion of the hot liquid was slowly added to increase the heat of the cold dairy or eggs so its temperature became more compatible with that of the hot liquid. Then the tempered mixture was added back to the hot liquid. If not tempered, the dairy product might tend to curdle or the eggs might cook. It was explained that to temper an item meant to stabilize it so its characteristics doesn't change when heated. This technique was also demonstrated for tempering chocolate where it was heated, then cooled, then heated again to stabilize the fat in the chocolate so it wouldn't crystallize once cooled. After further study, I realized that the process of tempering not only applied to food, but also cast iron, glass, steel and many other products to make them more resistant to stress. Again, the process involved heating the material to a certain temperature for a specific length of time and then rapidly cooling it to a normal temperature within a set time period.

All this talking about food stimulated not only my taste buds, but my thinking about the idea of tempering as it applies to our spiritual walk and relationship with one another. In Galatians 5:22-23 we see temperance listed among the nine fruit of the spirit as we read, *But the fruit of the Spirit is love, joy, peace, longsuffering, gentleness, goodness, faith, meekness, temperance: against such there is no law.* There may be situations where we find ourselves heated in our flesh, but we must not allow our Godly character to be compromised. Don't be quick or rash to go all in to the heat of the situation whereby you might curdle, cook, brew, stew or become unstable. Allow the Spirit of God to temper you and bring a calm, cool and spirit of peace to the matter so that you maintain your stability of character in Him.

Remember the Word of God does say in Ephesians 4:26, *Be ye angry, and sin not: let not the sun go down upon your wrath: Neither give place to the devil.* So, be stabilized in Godly character to help avoid any change in who you are in Christ when heated.

Sure Up

Be careful of the little foxes that spoil the vines, the deer that snip the leaves, birds that take flight with the fruit, the critter that swipes the eggs, or the beast that terrorizes the herd. Living in the country might afford more opportunity for creatures of the woods to venture onto your farm, your pasture, your garden area and cause reason for concern. But to our surprise, my mom experienced such an encounter living in the city. She had planted some sweet potato vines in a little garden spot next to the side of my home, nurtured and watched them grow and admired their lush green leaves and vines spreading themselves over the black earth. One evening she walked out only to find the leaves had been cut back. We thought perhaps the mowers had mistaken the vine for a weed when cutting the lawn the day before.

After a few days, the leaves started to grow back and my mom kept a watchful eye on their growth. She weeded the garden spot and pulled soil up around the vines to ensure that the mowers recognized that it was not a weed after all. The mowers came back and again the day after, my mom checked to again find the leaves cut back. Well, this time, we called a fellow gardener, my brother, to investigate the situation. He told us that deer were the culprits. He spotted their tracks and the mystery was solved. We learned that the leaves snipped from the vines stunted the growth of the sweet potato. And sure enough, later, when my mom dug under the vines, she found only thumb-sized would-be sweet potatoes. We baked and ate them.

I'd heard tales of dismay that other gardeners experienced. While at the peak of harvest, plans had been made to gather the yield but to awaken and find the vines or plants stripped of fruit; robbed of yield. No fruit to show for all of the labor. That image cannot only be disheartening, disappointing, discouraging, but vexation to your spirit. Though the culprit may have been some of God's lovely creatures, that thought does not lessen the loss. So how do you sure up to protect your person and your property from creatures of nature ravaging the works of all your hard labor? Some have put up fences and applied scents to which the creature had an aversion to while others have deployed strategies that we won't mention.

Let's consider the question from a spiritual perspective. How do we sure up our spiritual well-being in the Christian faith walk? There is so much that can be said. Addressed here are just some of the many strategies that can be utilized towards this end. Guard your heart and mind that ye may be able to stand against the wiles of the devil. Ephesians 6:11-18 instructs us to, *Put on the whole armour of God, that ye may be able to stand against the wiles of the devil. For we wrestle not against flesh and blood, but against principalities, against powers, against the rulers of the darkness of this world, against spiritual wickedness in high places. Wherefore take unto you the whole armour of God, that ye may be able to withstand in the evil day, and having done all, to stand. Stand therefore, having your loins girt about with truth, and having on the breastplate of righteousness; And your feet shod with the preparation of the gospel of peace, Above all, taking the shield of faith, wherewith ye shall be able to quench all the fiery darts of the wicked. And take the helmet of salvation, and the sword of the Spirit, which is the word of God: Praying always with all prayer and supplication in the Spirit, and watching thereunto with all perseverance and supplications for all saints...*

Yes, as Christians we know that we are covered under the blood of Jesus that was shed for us. He is our advocate with the Father God. We must also watch as well as pray. We send up the sweet smelling aroma of praise and worship to God as we enter into His gates with thanksgiving and into His courts with praise. As we enter into the Holy of Holies, we allow the peace of God to keep our hearts and minds. No, we don't want anything spoiling the fruit of our vines or terrorizing our hearts. So, be sure to Sure Up.

The Seed, The Sower

God gives seed to the sower. If you want/need seed, you must sow. It's the tried, true and tested way ordained by God Himself. He gave (sowed) His only begotten Son that there would be many sons (seed). All of us have been given something to sow. No exceptions! We have probably heard at some time in our lives, "I don't have it" or maybe we have even thought or voiced it ourselves. But the truth of the matter is, "Yes, we do have it." Perhaps, we have said, "This is my last" as the widow woman of Zarephath did in I Kings 17 when she answered the prophet Elijah who asked for a morsel of bread, *I have not a cake, but an handful of meal in a barrel, and a little oil in a cruise: and behold I am gathering two sticks, that I may go in and dress it for me and my son, that we may eat it, and die.* At the prophet's request, the widow woman sowed her last, "the little cake given to the prophet, Elijah first" and then she received the seed, for we read further in I Kings 17:15, *And she went and did according to the saying of Elijah: and she, and he, and her house, did eat many days.*

If we have an earnest desire to sow and seek God's direction, surely He will reveal the seed. It's in the house, within you, within your possession; and God has empowered you to get it in your hand and sow, that you might have seed. I reiterate here that "God gives seed to the sower." We must first have a willing mind to receive the promise of Isaiah 1:19, *If ye be willing and obedient, ye shall eat the good of the land...* Remember, we all have something to sow. We all do! Whatever your something is, entrust it from your hand to the Master's hand. As we sow, it is God that brings forth, gives the increase. Power, Peace and Prosperity are in your hands this day. As you sow your seed, God gives more seed. Start planting! A harvest is waiting! Sow, Seed, Repeat! It's the law of planting and reaping, not only in the natural, but also in the spirit.

Who Do You Know?

At mid-term one school year, I was assigned to work with a fifth grade class. There had been issues with the students and the instructor. Problems with student behavior had become common. Students had shown little growth academically which reflected in low test scores and grades. The class lagged behind the other fifth grade sections.

There was much work to be done and starting at mid-term made the task even more challenging. I was not too keen on the idea but I was committed to the work. The staff and school administrators welcomed me to the school and supported me in working with the class. The classroom had been newly set. The door was freshly done with my name included, much to my surprise. Meetings were held with the students outlining the change and expectations for improvement in all areas. Staff support was made available to provide needed assistance.

In my first meeting with the students, I assured them of my commitment to do and give them my best; and, likewise, my expectation from them to give and do their best. I explained the need for all of us to work together in order to move forward with a focus on improving grades and showing growth, and allowed them the time to express their concerns and ask questions. One question of major concern to students was how I would react to someone throwing something at me in the classroom.

It became evident that this had obviously been an issue for the previous teacher. While this was not alarming to me, I knew that I needed the Holy Spirit to speak through me in answer to their question. He did. I took a panoramic snapshot of the class as I looked intently into the eyes of each student. Then, speaking in my lower registered sure but firm voice, responded "I am not afraid of any one of you and I am not concerned about any of you throwing anything at me, because I know someone who will take care of me. And if you do, I know someone who will take care of you." A holy hush came over that class. During my limited service assignment, I can tell you that the action in question never happened.

Those students tugged on my heart strings daily and I spent much time in prayer for them. I went to the altar for them many times and, yes, anointed the classroom. We faced many challenges, but we finished the year strong and realized positive growth both in grades and character development.

For all the teachers out there, be encouraged, fear not and walk in the authority given you for the scriptures reminds us in I John 4:4 that, *Ye are of God, little children, and have overcome them: because greater is He that is in you, than he that is in the world.* Ephesians 6:10 also commends us, *Finally, my breth-*

ren, be strong in the Lord, and in the power of His might. Put on your whole armour. Furthermore, God will provide a refreshing for He lets us know in Isaiah 40:31, *But they that wait upon the Lord shall renew their strength; they shall mount up with wings as eagles; they shall run, and not be weary; and they shall walk, and not faint.* When "You Know" Him, you are empowered and equipped to do all that God has given your hands to do.

He Loves Me

As giggly young adolescences or teens, we might have sometimes played the game, "He loves me, He loves me not." With dreamy eyes, butterfly flutters and our beau in mind, we pluck the first petal from a most delicate flower saying, "He love me" and then pluck the next petal saying, "He loves me not." That continues until the last petal with the hopes of it being "He loves me." We all want to be loved whether we admit it or not. With God, we don't have to ask or question His love for us because that's who God is— God is Love.

Does the sun ever stop shining or the moon forbids its glow?

Do the trees stop swaying when the great winds blow?

So is God's love commended towards us don't you know?

He's ever with us no matter where we go.

If we go to the depths of the deep blue sea

*Or we look out over the vast expanse of the
ocean wide, He is there.*

*If we go to the highest mountain top or to
infinity and beyond, He is there.*

__Rose Sutton

The question is asked in Psalm 139:7, *Whither shall I go from Thy spirit? or whither shall I flee from Thy presence?* It continues in verses 8-12, *If I ascend up into heaven, Thou art there: if I make my bed in hell, behold, Thou art there. If I take the wings of the morning, and dwell in the uttermost parts of the sea; Even there shall Thy hand lead me, and Thy right hand shall hold me. If I say, Surely the darkness shall cover me; even the night shall be light about me. Yea, the darkness hideth not from Thee; but the night shineth as the day: the darkness and the light are both alike to Thee.*

God's love permeates all. It finds us where we are, and we are enveloped in the blanket of His love when we open our hearts to Him. He is patiently waiting. He Loves You! He Loves You! He Loves Me!

Catch On Fire

Most of us can recall our experience as a New Christian—the love we felt, the thirst for more of God's Spirit and the desire to be filled with His Joy and Peace. The zeal for service and desire to please Him were all a part of the newness of life that we felt. For me, it was like discovering a whole new world that changed my perspective on life. People would often describe their new birth experience in song. They would sing, *I looked at my hands and they looked new, I looked at my feet and they did too.* I've heard some say that the grass looked greener, the birds chirping sounded sweeter, the sky was bluer and brighter. God's Word does say in 2 Corinthians 5:17, *Therefore if any man be in Christ, he is a new creature: old things are passed away; behold, all things are become new.* My desire and hunger was to learn and know Him more. Whatever gifts awaiting me from the Father, I wanted. Thus, began my adventure in Him.

Baptism in Him, an outward act of the inner heart experience was a natural course of order to follow as a profession of my faith. Jesus charged His disciples in Matthew 28:19 to, *Go ye therefore, and teach all nations, baptizing them in the name of the Father, and of the Son, and of the Holy Ghost...* Acts 2:38 records, *Then Peter said unto them, Repent, and be baptized every one of you in the name of Jesus Christ for the remission of sins, and ye shall receive the gift of the Holy Ghost.* Romans 6:3-4 further explains, *Know ye not, that so many of us as were baptized into Jesus Christ were baptized into His death? Therefore we are buried with Him by baptism into death: that like as Christ was raised up from the dead by the glory of the Father, even so we also should walk in newness of life.* Reading Galatians 3:27 which affirms that, *For as many of you as have been baptized into Christ have put on Christ* assured me that baptism was indeed an expression of what I longed for.

I'm reminded of those infomercials on TV that state, "but wait, there's more." So, upon further study of God's Word, I came to understand that Jesus promised the gift of His Holy Spirit and to be filled with His Spirit as on the Day of Pentecost in the upper room experience. While some ministries may not provide much teaching on this, I am an inquisitive Child of God and I wanted to know about all that He had and has for me. God spoke in Matthew 5:6 that, *Blessed are they which do hunger and thirst after righteousness: for they shall be filled.* And I can tell you that the in-filling of His Spirit is real for all who believe with the evidence of Speaking in Tongues, that heavenly language given by God. Give yourself and be open to all God's wonderful gifts. They are for our edification. His offer given in Matthew 7:7 to, *Ask, and it shall be given you; seek, and ye shall find; knock, and it shall be opened unto you:* does not just pertain to natural things, but spiritual things as well. He goes on say in Verse 8 that, *For every one that asketh receiveth;*

and he that seeketh findeth; and to him that knocketh it shall be opened. Filled, I am and happily so. It's humbling, but so rewarding. Seek God's leading, read and study the Book of Acts for a more in-depth study of this gift.

Continue your study in His Word that you go to those deeper depths and higher heights in Him. Let it be your heart's throb to know Him more and more going from faith to faith and glory to glory. Catch on fire and spread the Word—The Good News of the Gospel of Jesus Christ.

Places Everyone

As a fellow thespian, I've had occasion to be on stage and off as an actor, director, part of tech crew and assistant. Doing so has given some insight and understanding to the operation and flow of theatrical work. In producing a play, the director has already concluded lots of work before the scene work and rehearsals begin. Let's start our overview here with a few elements relative to the scene work. Once all cast members receive their scripts, they should, of course, read through and start to learn the lines. One should also study the character's nature and traits—how he moves, the subtleties, the nuances to the point that you become that character—but only for the run of the play. You should become familiar with the staging or blocking. Know how, where, and when you are to move. Be careful not to upstage or step on someone else's lines, nor stand in the line of another character. And, by all means, never turn your back to the audience when speaking. There may be a rare time, however, that the director gives permission for that. But again, it's rare.

Now, if you don't quite understand what's being said to this point, I take liberty here to invite you to join a theatre group or even the JRC theatre group to get in on all the fun. Call me!

Let's get back to the script. While in rehearsal, scenes are often repeated. This allows actors to further develop their character and the inter-workings and relationships with fellow actors on the stage. Sometimes this process may take a while because we want to give and be our best on the stage. As sound, lights, and props are added to further enhance the work, we must make any necessary adjustments to adapt. The desire is to draw and capture the audience's attention engaging them into believing the realness of the scene. That will be the gauge of a job well done.

It's now time for dress rehearsal and actors are attired in full costume. I've found that things seem to come alive when cast members come together in full garb, under the lights, props at the ready, and on the sound enhanced stage. Electricity seems to fill the air as the actors take their places and the culmination of all the hard work is revealed on stage.

As Christians, we should daily read our script, the Word of God, and commit it onto the tables of our hearts. We are to *Study to shew thyself approved unto God, a workman that needeth not to be ashamed, rightly dividing the word of truth,* as charged in 2 Timothy 2:15. Learn the character of Christians and ascribe to reflect Christ in our lives each day as we interact with our fellowman, God's creation. We might consider this as character development. Be sensitive to the Holy Spirit that leads and directs our movements. Follow directions!

Remember, all that we do should give glory and honor to God and not ourselves. We lift Him up and He will draw by His Spirit as Jesus spoke in John 12:32, *And I, if I be lifted up from the earth, will draw all men unto me.* Utilize the gifts God gives unto your hands. Walk in the light as He is the light. Watch for the signals that He gives. Listen when He speaks to your heart. It may be a gentle whisper. He has told us in John 10:27, *My sheep hear my voice, and I know them, and they follow me...* We put on the whole armour of God as given in Ephesians 6:11-18. We are clothed upon with righteousness as described in Isaiah 61:10, *I will greatly rejoice in the Lord, my soul shall be joyful in my God; for He hath clothed me with the garments of salvation, and He hath covered me with the robe of righteousness, as a bridegroom decketh himself with ornaments, and as a bride adorneth herself with her jewels.*

On stage, when the last line has been delivered and applause and encores rendered, the actors bow in acceptance of the appreciation for their work. With God, when we finish our course, it's our delight to hear Him say as in Matthew 25:21... *Well done, thou good and faithful servant: thou hast been faithful over a few things, I will make thee ruler over many things: enter thou into the joy of Thy Lord.* But at the end of time when our Lord, The Director returns, we understand *That at the name of Jesus every knee should bow, of things in heaven, and things in earth, and things under the earth. And that every tongue should confess that Jesus Christ is Lord, to the glory of God the Father,* as proclaimed in Philippians 2:10-11. Glory Be to God! Hallelujah! Now, Places Everybody!

Twinkle, Twinkle Little Star

Traditionally, on July 4th in the United States, people celebrate Independence Day with lots of firework displays. Eyes light up and a sense of awe fill our hearts as we behold the magnificent array of lights in the night sky. Some might even engage in friendly neighborhood fireworks competitions to see who has the biggest bang or brightest broadcast lighting up the night. The bursts of glorious light cascades just have a way of capturing our attention whether we are near or far. We gaze at the sky and give wondrous applause as we marvel at such displays. Our eyes twinkle in the light's glow.

Though the fireworks enthrall us with dazzling light displays, how much more are we called to be lights in a dark world? We understand from Genesis 1, that in the beginning, gross darkness covered the face of the earth and God spoke light into it. When God created man in His image and blew His breath into man, He blew life and light, because... *God is light, and in Him is no darkness at all* as declared to us in 1 John 1:5. As children of God, we are the children of light. However, 1 John 1:6-7 continues, *If we say that we have fellowship with Him, and walk in darkness, we lie, and do not the truth: But if we walk in the light, as He is in the light, we have fellowship one with another, and the blood of Jesus Christ His Son cleanseth us from all sin.* Children of God, walk in the light.

We are that city spoken of in Matthew 5:14-16—a city set on a hill whose light cannot be hid. Ye are the light of the world. There are souls depending on our light to see the way out of darkness. We are to let our lights so shine before men that they may see the glorious love of God and be drawn to Him. He is the Light of the World. He has given us that light, and we are to fulfill our commission to lift up our lights through love so that others may be drawn to the light and see Jesus. The time is now. Souls are in the balance, and it just might be that someone is depending on you to cast light that they may see the way out of darkness.

My fellow labors in Christ, "Be that light today," whether at home, workplace, school, community or wherever life's path takes you. The light of your life can twinkle, twinkle like a star in praise to Him as well. Heavenly Father, in that day of your return, our desire is to be found faithful. Help us to be of that heart and mind.

Contributing Writers

Hospital Visitor

After the last of my last of six children was born, I became ill a few weeks before Christmas. A local hospital treated and discharged me, but there was no improvement. My husband was doing what he could to care for the children and attend to me. The hospital staff informed us that it would take some time for the medication to take effect, but my condition had only grown worse. After speaking with an out of town relative, my husband decided to transfer me to another hospital that might be better equipped. Plans were made to transport me the next day, but I told him that I felt so sick I didn't know if I would make it to the next morning. A neighbor helped to put me in the car and he drove me that night to the other hospital. The hospital admitted me and administered a series of tests. The results showed no evidence of the condition for which I had been treated at the local hospital. I was given a solution to drink, but my body would not tolerate the liquid. Another patient that had been in the room with me, but was moved and I was left alone. It appeared as if the hospital attendants had sectioned me off from the other patients. My condition was grave. I heard hushed whispers and it seemed that I had been given up on and wasn't expected to make it through the night. While

I lay there, I began to pray and ask God to heal me. It was then that I felt God's presence fill the room. The Spirit of God spoke to me and said, "You're not going to die, you have some work to do." That hospital visitor was the Great Physician. At that moment, I did not know what God had for me to do, but I did know that His Word was and is real.

My condition improved and I was soon discharged for the hospital, completely made whole. Yes, I most certainly did live and began a life of work and service to the Lord. Since that time I have worked in different areas of ministry in my home, in my church, and in my community doing whatever God gave unto my hands to do. The work has spanned over sixty years. With each opportunity to minister, I am ever mindful to thank God for life and health. I thank Him for the work He has given my hands to do as teacher, singer, intercessor, leader, encourager, and servant in any way He needs me. My desire is to live and continue working while it is day doing that which is in accordance to God's Word, His Will, and His Way. All praises to God for His hospital visit and granting me a life's work that has been both rewarding and fulfilling.

Inez B. Sutton

Miracle Through the Eyes of a Child

Growing up as a child, I recall times with family, playing with friends, going to school, going to church and Sunday School, and just plain old having fun. But then, one day I began to experience soreness in my throat. At first, I did not give much attention to it, but after a day or so, a fever developed. My parents took a long look at my throat and decided I needed to be taken to a throat doctor. After taking cultures and other tests, the doctors informed my parents of my condition and suggested a series of treatments. After treatments, I got better, but then began to get worse. We began to visit the doctor's office frequently, and then one day I remember vividly the doctor telling my parents that the treatments were not going to cure my condition and that they needed to have my tonsils removed.

I thought, "I don't want my tonsils taken out." Although I remember having a personal experience with the Lord, as a child, I didn't recall at the time any scripture for believing God for a MIRACLE. I just began to pray unto the Lord my own child's prayer, "Lord, all the other children have tonsils and I want mine too." That was all I prayed. Let me tell you, that was all it took. By the way, no one but God and I knew the prayer that I had prayed. The doctors scheduled me to have my tonsils removed the following week, but I believed God for that MIRACLE.

Our church was in a revival during that week prior to my scheduled procedure. My parents attended the revival on Friday night (the last night of the revival). Some of my older siblings stayed home with me. I lay in bed with chills, fever, and infection. My parents returned from the revival service and the Preacher/Prophet/Gift of Healing was with them. They had opened our home to him and invited him to stay with us. My mom asked him to pray for me during his stay with us. He came into the room and laid hands on me in faith (believing) for my healing and at that very hour, I was instantly healed miraculously until this very day. This was a miracle through the Eyes of a Child as I remembered it. To God Be The Glory For The Things He Has Done and What A Mighty God We Serve!

Cynthia Smith

Redeemed

My dreams and hopes for a "happy ever after" were shattered when my husband and I divorced. Our two children were in my care and it became increasingly difficult providing for them and keeping a roof over our heads. The house payments were behind and I didn't know what to do. I decided to refinance the mortgage loan to make things more manageable. Things seemed to be going well for about three years until the day when a man came to our door and presented papers saying he owned our home. He said that the home had been bought for unpaid taxes on the home over the last three years. Not being keen on business matters, I came to realize that when the home was refinanced, taxes were not included in the mortgage payment. It was as if my home had been stolen from me. The man offered to let us stay in the house while paying rent. So we did that for a while. Though my heart was broken, I stood fast in prayer and knew that somehow, someway we were going to get our home back. That was my daily confession. I knew God would lead me and show me what to do, that He would work by His Spirit on my behalf. Even when others who were aware of the situation would say there was no way I would get the house back, I would always say, "God is going to get me my house back." I continued to pray. As time went on, at the suggestion of a friend who knew about the matter, I consulted a mortgage attorney. The attorney contacted me after looking through the papers and found that the home had been illegally taken from me because I had not been served the proper papers prior to the home being sold for taxes. He told me the bank would have to give me the house back. When all was said and done, God did just what I confessed and believed for. In fact, He did exceeding, abundantly, above all I could ever ask or think. The house was given back to me without a mortgage. Yes, from homeless to home free (a home without a mortgage). Hallelujah! I just praise God! I just praise Him! God gave me my house back. Yes, He did.

Nora Hayes

My Miracle

In 2003 I began to experience pain in my lower stomach about the same time each month and thought it to be associated with my cycle. The pain began to be more intense and after a year of enduring the discomfort, I consulted my OBGYN. She referred me for a CT scan of my abdomen. The scan revealed a mass on my ovary. At that point she indicated that a biopsy needed to be ordered to check for cancer. I looked at her and replied, "It's not cancer." She gave me a strange look and asked, "Ms. Norton. What did you say?" I repeated, "It's not cancer." The OBGYN then responded, "Okay, but just get the biopsy." I told her that I would.

Later, while driving to work, the adversary began to whisper thoughts that it was cancer. I quickly had to dismiss those thoughts. My daughter's face flashed before me and I began to cry. I desired to be around to care for her. My Aunt and I agreed in prayer decreeing God's Word and proclaiming the blood of Jesus over the situation prior to the test.

I must admit that I was a bit nervous about things, but knew God to be faithful. The results came back just as I spoke to my OBGYN—Not cancer. Praise God! A procedure was scheduled to remove the mass and possibly the ovaries as well. I consented and again prayed God's Word.

Again I was a bit apprehensive about being put to sleep and being operated on, but having my mom with me was comforting. Aside from that, I can remember the anesthesiologist singing to me while I was going under his rendition of a Willie Nelson's song Of All the Girls I've Loved Before. God is so Good.

When waking up I heard babies crying, but knew I surely didn't have a baby. Then I heard my daughter's voice calling me. I looked at her and asked, "Where am I?" She smiled and responded, "You're on the maternity floor."

The doctor come around later and said, "Ms. Norton, you are a blessed woman. That mass we saw was your appendix. It had ruptured and grew over your ovary that had to be removed. I don't know how you were able to endure the pain for as long as you did." I knew that it was all God. My God is an awesome God! I know that God works miracles and I am living proof.

Tracy Norton

Rigged Blessings

In the early years of my marriage, my husband and I pinched pennies to make ends meet. There was only money for the basic things. We both were faithful in our local church and believed in prayer. On a Friday night during one church revival, I went to the altar for prayer, anointing and blessings. The next morning my mother-in-law was going to the nearby town and asked if I would go with her. We stopped in at the bank for her to conduct some transactions. While there, one of the bank tellers told us that the town was celebrating Harvest Day and invited us to sign up for the drawings being held during the day. We did, of course. I went on to stop by the grocery store because I needed some washing powder to wash our family's clothes. I had just enough money for that. But I saw a ham that I wanted, but knew I did not have the money for both. In my heart I wanted the ham, but knew the washing powder was needed and I could only get that. I walked around the store thinking about the ham, when I heard my name called out to come to the front of the store. My name had been drawn for a cash prize on Harvest Day and now I had enough money for the washing powder, ham and more. Praise God!

My mother-in-law left the grocery store and stopped by another. Not long after we had stepped inside the store, my name was called again to receive another cash prize. Praise God! Praise God! Praise God! Glory! We decided to stop by another store, and again my name was drawn for a cash prize. Let me tell you I know that God will indeed supply all of your needs according to his riches in glory. We went to another store, but I was told if my name was drawn again, I would not be able to receive the cash prize because others might think the drawings were somehow rigged. I watched as they drew the next name from the box. Well, wouldn't you know, they put the slip with the name back in the box and drew another. If you ask me, that Harvest Day was rigged just for me. God had answered my prayer and blessed me indeed.

Inez B. Sutton

In Spite of My Youth

And the child grew and became strong; he was filled with wisdom, and the grace of God was on him. Luke 2:40 (NIV)

I had a hunch that I was going to be moving soon, but I didn't know where. I loved my apartment. Nevertheless, I knew in my spirit it was time to move. "Not into another apartment, but a home," said the Lord to my soul. You see, there is a difference between a house and a home. A house is a place of occupancy. A home, on the other hand, is filled with love and peace, and it permeates the atmosphere of a place making it a harbor of love. I like to think of a home as a house with more depth. It's a place that satisfies your soul, an area of personality, a place where people feel safe and welcome when they visit. It's a place of my own personal space and I was ready to possess that space.

Though I naturally couldn't see how things were going to work out in my favor, I believed God. I was only twenty-six at the time; I was still young. I had a lot to learn. Was I ready to handle all of the responsibilities connected with home ownership? "Well, if God said move, then I must move, and He will make the way," I thought. Shortly after that conversation, God did just that!

One evening I was watching television and saw a real estate commercial. There it was—the home I was to occupy. I called my agent and told her about the listing. We scheduled to see the house the next day. When I walked through the front door, there was such a sense of peace I had not felt with any other properties I had seen. Since God had shown me the home, how was I to possess the land? He knew I would have questions and I knew He would have the answers.

In spite of having made some poor money management choices that caused me to have a poor credit score, God was gracious towards me. He gave me wisdom, strategies, and resources to get out of debt much faster than what others projected. He spoke to someone's heart to bless me with the escrow money, and I was also blessed with appliances to go in my new home. All of this was done without me paying a dime. I am so grateful.

There were many naysayers. They even voiced their doubts. But I held fast in my faith and confessed, "WHAT GOD HAD FOR ME, WAS FOR ME!" And on June 9th while yet in my 20s, the prime of my youth, I stood in my new home. I was the homeowner of my new home that had been completed by the builders only a few months before my move-in date.

I believe God had signed the deed to this home in the beginning of time as one of His good and perfect gifts for me. Now all I needed to do was sign my name, receive it and give Him all the glory. In spite of my youth and the obstacles that were encountered, God proved himself strong on my behalf. He was and IS Ephesians 3:20! I will forever give Him all the praise!

Dr. Tracey Bell Jernigan

He Is My Provider

Now unto him who is able to do exceeding abundantly above all that we can ask or think, according to the power that worketh in us... as referenced in Ephesians 3:20 attests to the power of God that will work in our lives when we believe and stand in faith.

My husband and I were young parents of four small children. He worked in a low-paying job at a warehouse while I taught at a local high school. We had experienced some severe financial difficulties that prompted us to declare bankruptcy. Even so, we barely had enough money between us to pay bills. Aside from that, our only means of transportation kept breaking down. Because of the recent bankruptcy and current financial situation, the thought of acquiring another vehicle seemed out of the question. Something had to be done though. It seemed that I was consistently late arriving for work due to the vehicle breaking down—almost three days out of the week. My principal and co-workers were understanding of our transportation situation, but we knew that could not go on. To make matters worse, our arrival at school was always announced with a great cloud of smoke and thunderous noise—talk about embarrassing and humiliating. Nevertheless, we kept plugging along.

I remember one morning awakening at the usual hour and a half before normal departure time to get everyone up and ready in order for me to hopefully arrive to work at a reasonable time. It was a cold, wintry, rainy morning. Let me note here that I was about five months pregnant. The car was put-putting along with its usual smoke and sputter. I dropped the youngest at day care and the three other children at their schools. I was just a couple of blocks from the high school where I worked. Just then, right in front of me a wheel was spinning down the street, and I was puzzled at the sight. At that moment my vehicle came to a jolting, screeching, thudding stop as I managed to steer it to the side of the road. It became clear that the tire had come from my car—the axle had broken on the front wheel.

I was shaken by the ordeal, but not hurt. You can believe me, I thanked God for His protection and His mercy. God had shielded me from what could have been a horrible wreck or serious accident. There were no other vehicles on what otherwise was a heavily trafficked street and my car had been safely steered away from the nearby trees while coming to a stop. Once out of the car, it began to drizzle and I began to cry. I so desperately needed God's intervention for I felt that I could go no further. So as I started the walk on to the school, I cried, prayed and reminded God of a dream that I felt He had given me a few months earlier. In the dream, I was taken to a beautiful house and given papers and keys to a car by a man I didn't know. I did not know how or when, but I believed God and told Him so. Still crying and praying, I made it to work at school just in time for the bell.

During my break, I went to call my husband from the teacher's lounge to let him know about the situation. Another teacher was on the phone so I just waited. Once off the phone, the teacher looked at me saying that God had placed me on her heart. She went on to say that she had spoken to a friend about my transportation situation. The friend knew someone who was planning on selling his wife's car because he had bought her a new jeep. Cost and other details about the car were not available as the owners were on vacation at the time. A spark of hope surged my being sensing that God was working on my behalf.

Time went by, but my husband and I stood in faith encouraging ourselves with the Word of God, especially Ephesians 3:20. It was about a month later the teacher who spoke with me in the lounge approached me breathless with excitement telling me that the owners of the car were still on vacation, but the man had contacted his Pastor, who happened to be the teacher's friend's husband to tell him of a dream he had. In his dream, God had instructed him not to sell the car, but to give it away and that He would make known just who it was to be given to once they returned from vacation. It so happened they were returning at the end of that week. That day the teacher and I sat in my classroom and agreed in prayer that God would have His way in the matter. That Friday, she came by my classroom to ask if she and her husband could come by to take my husband and I to meet the owners of the car. Of course, we said "Yes".

We drove up to an area of gated mansions that I never knew existed in our area. With wide-eyes and wonder, we kept driving until coming to what seemed to be the largest of the mansions. Yes, this was the house. We drove down the enormous driveway and saw a beautiful blue Ford Taurus station wagon sitting there as we turned into the driveway. The owner and his wife walked out to greet us as we walked up. They directed us to the garage where there were two beautiful cars and a Jeep inside. There was also the one that we saw driving up outside of the garage. The owner told us himself of his dream and his first thoughts of donating the car to a charity as a tax write-off, but that God had tugged at his heart and troubled him in his sleep. When he called the friend's husband, he knew what God had directed him to do.

At that point, he and his wife invited us into the home, and we all sat down at their breakfast table. Yes, God had spoken to his heart to give us the car—the beautiful blue Ford Taurus Station Wagon. It was a 1989, fully loaded vehicle with new tires and low mileage. You see, it was 1990 when my husband and I sat at that breakfast table and signed the papers that the owner had already drawn up and ready for us. He handed us the keys and walked us out to our new car. At that moment, my dream flashed before me. Yes, it was the dream God had given me of being taken to a beautiful house where a man handed me papers and the keys to a new car. My friend's husband who had driven us to meet the owner turned to my husband and said, *Now unto him that is able to do exceeding abundantly above all that we ask or think, according to the power that worketh in us.* Ephesians 3:20. My husband could no longer contain himself. When he heard those words, the spirit of the Lord filled that driveway and he shouted right then and there.

God had seen my tears, He had heard my prayers, He had spoken to a man who knew nothing about us, He had given me a dream, He had given the man a dream and, yes, God had brought the dream to pass as we continued in faith. The Father God had given my husband and I the papers and the keys to our new car—no charge. We drove from that place shouting and giving God all glory. God's love is great to all. God is our provider and when we tell you that He is able to do just what Ephesians 3:20 says, believe it! There is nothing too hard for our God!

Cordelia Godfrey

God is a Great and Glorious God!

He has done such magnificent feats such that the world cannot contain the magnitude of His wonderful works. I give Him all Glory! He is the True and Living and Only God!

Many years ago when I was younger in life and in my walk with the Lord, I recall an awesome way He moved to help in a mighty way. My brother and a couple of other men had arrived from college around 2 a.m. in the morning to rest for a few hours before leaving on a flight for summer army training. They had nearly overslept and we had rushed as quickly as we could to the airport. Pressing their way in as much timeliness they could muster to get to the check-in counter, the young army hopefuls were informed by the attendant they had just missed their flight. Feeling devastated, they stepped away and began looking out the window and could see the plane beginning to back out. Inside I felt faith arise as I remembered as we were driving the Lord had given me a strong witness that they would not miss the flight. We had arrived at the airport with a sense of urgency knowing that it would be a close call and a great possibility of being too late. I began praising the Lord deep inside myself. And in as brief a moment as the attendant had said the flight was missed, she beckoned for the young men to return to the counter and get checked in. The attendant explained there was something on the plane that needed to be rechecked and it would give them just enough time to board. They boarded the plane, did not miss the flight and nothing was wrong with the plane upon checking. The Hand of the Lord had moved in this situation and the victory He had declared truly came to pass! There is no one like our Lord and none can do what only He can. All Power is given unto Him! Hallelujah!

Hattie Peyton

Rejoice In Everything

I've faced many challenges during my lifetime. But there's one that challenged the very core of my being—my faith in God. During one of my routine self-breast exams, I felt a lump and scheduled an exam with my doctor. It was confirmed and I was referred to a specialist. A needle biopsy was ordered, but did not reveal anything. This was seemingly "Good News," but the specialist, however, insisted on an incision biopsy. The results revealed cancer that was behind a mass. Even in that, I thanked God that it had been detected early and not dismissed because of the mass.

Though the news was not what I desired, I could only hear the Father God saying to my spirit to "rejoice in all things, and again I say rejoice." Mind you, this was not easy. But during the process of it all, those were the words that rang in my ears. The next step in my journey was surgery. The surgery was scheduled and God blessed me with the finest surgeon who removed several lump nodules. The nodules were free of cancer and had not spread. Praise God!

After being hospitalized and undergoing surgical procedures for three days, I was discharged. This too was remarkable. I was in Church the following Sunday rejoicing in my spirit and praising God.

The course of my journey was one shared with those of my family and the team which I led during my military tenure. All were supportive. My team was a bit sad, shedding tears at first. But the Lord strengthened me to strengthen them. God's Spirit always gently whispered, "rejoice in everything." God had given me an amazing Word of comfort and strength that kept me in faith all along the journey. His Word found in 1 Thessalonians 5:16-18 that says *Rejoice evermore. Pray without ceasing. In every thing give thanks: for this is the will of God in Christ Jesus concerning you* is a Sustaining Word. It has kept me throughout my life.

Yes, it's easy to rejoice when things are going well, but God blessed me to understand that I can rejoice in Him even so when receiving a diagnosis like cancer. I thank God for His Word and allowing me to be a witness to others of His Power and Grace having gone through the cancer. Yes, it was a test that gave me a testimony. God is So Good! Give Him praise... *for we know that all things work together for good to them that love God, to them who are the called according to His purpose* as we are assured in Romans 8:28. Rejoice in Him today through the bad and the good.

Colonel (Retired) Alma J. Miller

A Time To Be Still

For years I had experienced excruciating headaches while sleeping only two or three hours each night, but pushing through to work eight to ten hours on my job. Sometimes I worked weekends too along with a part-time job. Aside from that, my parents had left me in charge of caring for a disabled brother which meant cooking, cleaning, shopping—among all the other caregiver responsibilities. Somehow I managed to keep up the routine day in and day out until in March 2017 my world as I knew it was abruptly interrupted.

It was on that day that my son noticed some rather strange behavior in responding to him. You see, he worked for the same company as I and had stopped by my area. He was so alarmed that he spoke with my supervisor and informed him that he was taking me to the hospital immediately. He then turned off my computer, threw my purse over his shoulder, put his arm around my waist leading me out to his car. During all of this I was fussing and saying that I wasn't going and had to finish work.

Nevertheless, we arrived at St. Dominic Hospital. There they quickly determined that I was having seizures. A CT scan was done on my head to reveal a massive brain tumor. The doctor advised me of the two choices before me. Either I could elect to have brain surgery to remove the tumor which would be risky or I could elect to do nothing in which case death would be impending due to the size of the tumor. He informed me that the tumor had grown so that it was pushing back on my brain so much so causing swelling and limiting the space for my brain. All of this brought me to my knees while crying in somewhat disbelief. But after some time of crying out to God, I consented to the surgery. The doctor then informed me that due to the extensive swelling in my head, I would be put on medication for a week or so just to reduce the swelling.

The procedure was scheduled for March 20, 2017 at 7:00 a.m. I can remember on that day, though I was prepped for the surgery, another patient was brought in at my scheduled time due to an emergency. I leaned that, sadly, the patient died on the operating table. At 1:00 p.m. that same day my procedure began and was completed at 11:50 p.m. After two weeks in the intensive care unit, I was moved to a room. Soon after, however, I was moved back to intensive care due to complications. The complications were such that my family was informed that my body organs were shutting down and it was just a matter of time. Beyond the facts of that situation, God's Truth prevailed and no, I did not die. I praise God for His Grace and Mercy. While yet hospitalized, the adversary brought thoughts of the still present situation. Knowing that the front of my head had been shaved from ear to ear, vision lost in my right eye, loss of my sense of smell and taste, high risk for seizures and blood clots, the costs and expense of the medical care, loss of wages while being on extended medical leave and whatever was of a dire nature all contributed to my becoming deeply depressed. I cried continuously at night feeling deep despair and loneliness.

I was highly sedated with medications for all of this, but still had the presence of mind to call out to my God. Hallelujah! Yes, the one thing I knew to do was pray and pour my heart out to God. I began to meditate and quote scriptures, the Word of God. As I prayed, I remember saying, Father, you said in your Word that you would not put more on us than we can bear, so I know I can bear this, but it's hard. Your Word says that you are my strength and my shield. Father, I need your strength now. I know that it was your Grace and Mercy that brought me to this point in life and I thank and praise you for everything. So, please help me know. I begin to cry uncontrollably. It was then I heard a voice at the foot of that hospital bed call my name twice. I looked and I knew it was the voice of God. He said to me, *Be still and know that I am God.* I lay there as God's presence filled me with a Peace that I had not known before. That Spoken Word had walked right in that room giving me comfort and letting me know that I need only be still and trust Him. Those Words changed not only my perspective of the situation, but my life.

After being hospitalized for several months, I continued treatment at Methodist Rehab Hospital for two weeks. I was discharged in mid-May 2017 to follow-up my medical treatment through intensive outpatient rehab several days each week. And even though there were lots of prescription meds to take, I have been blessed to discontinue some because the health issue no longer exists. Praise God! In addition, I experienced tremendous weight loss going from a size 20 to a size 10. Again, Praise God!

It has been a yearlong journey, but I'm here to tell you that My God has been and is faithful. The Lord has held my hand tightly this past year, and oftentimes He carried me over the steep hills and across the valleys. I must stop right here and say, "Thank You Lord!" I have been released by the doctor to return to work March 2018. What a Mighty God we serve!

I learned that the Lord may permit obstacles along our path sometimes for our own good. You see, it is through those obstacles that we grow—we grow in faith, we grow in the Word, and we learn how to lean on and trust our Heavenly Father Even The More.

We serve An Awesome God, A Forgiving God, A Patient God, A Loving God, A Healing God. He is My Perfect Father. He's my mother, brother, sister and friend. He is my EVERYTHING! Thank You Father and I forever praise your Name.

Your Child,
Essie Williams

About the Contributing Writers

Cordelia Godfrey is an educator, artesian and writer. She has served in public education for over 30 years and acknowledges that to be her calling. She also ministers alongside her husband and they both share the joy of children and grands.

Nora Hayes knows the power of prayer and faithfully attends early morning 5:30am prayer. She proudly acknowledges her status as mother, grandmother and great grandmother. Nora enjoys her retirement years shopping and spending time with family and friends. She exudes a joyful spirit to all she meets.

Dr. Tracey Bell Jernigan has served in education for at least fifteen years and continues to spread the love of Christ through educating others. She is a life-long learner who enjoys spending time with her husband, family and friends. She enjoys cooking, traveling and participating in painting classes.

Alma J. Miller, retired Colonel of the U.S. Airforce, after serving nearly 30 years has continued Federal Service for over 10 years in the Cyber Security Field. She credits her success as a commander in the military and all other aspects of her life to her acknowledgment of Jesus Christ as her Lord and Savior.

Tracy Norton spent over 20 years as Food Service Director for a Correctional Facility where she gladly shared her faith with those she served. She currently serves as Nutrition Manager in the public school system. As a mother and grandmother, her heart's desire is to be a light of God's love to her family and all she meets that souls would be saved.

Hattie Peyton ministers the love of God in word, prayer and praise. Worship flows through her being in dance to give God glory! Her love of Jesus transcends into love for family and people as she lives seeking and seeing the Lord heal and save His people.

Cynthia Smith wife and mother of five beautiful children, is passionate about her walk with the Lord. Degreed in accounting, she served in state service for nearly fifteen years. She currently gives herself to ministry in her home and attributes all glory to God for a life of faith, hope, perseverance and trust in Him.

Inez B. Sutton shares a wealth of wisdom from her walk with the Lord to her children, grandchildren and great grandchildren. Thanking God for her 88 years, she continues to impart and instruct, love and serve as God so commissioned.

Essie Williams has tenure with Eaton Aerospace that spans over 42 years. She willingly gives herself to serving others and knows God's power that has strengthened and sustained her throughout her life's journey.

Acknowledgments

With a grateful heart, I extend expressions of thanks to all those who share the joy of this work with me.

Estella, "editor in chief" you are appreciated much more than you know for all the time spent and expertise given to at long last help me share this work in print. May God's favor ever rest upon you. Love ya my friend.

Jeff and Tonja, thank you for doing what you do so well in mentoring, caring and, sharing your talents with those of us who lean more to the creative rather than tech aspect of things.

Thanks to the contributing writers who were willing to share accounts of God's divine intervention in their lives giving testament to the power of God in a time of need.

The JRC Ministry staff holds a special place in my heart. The Spirit of God, without a doubt, graciously led me those many years ago to this place rich in God's love and grace. I am forever grateful for the expressions of love and care given while nurturing my spiritual growth and maturity in Christ.

Pastor Jennifer, I am in awe of God's love to have so graced my life with the rare and precious gift of your being. My heart wells with gratefulness and appreciation when I reflect on the wonder of it all. I am humbled and honored by the giving of your time, your person, your blessing to this work. I Love You!

I don't take it lightly to have been blessed with Christian parents who loved me, supported and encouraged me, lived a life before me and taught me Christian values. I Love YOU!

All glory to God for divine inspiration and stirrings to expressions. Thank you for your unconditional love for me.

About The Author

The author, LINDA ROSE SUTTON, a native Mississippi-an, reflected on her rich life experiences and Christian heritage to pen the collection of inspirational short stories, Reflections, Recollections Revelations. She delightfully recounts many lessons learned through her adventures and experiences that attest to the power of God's written, spoken and living Word. Her writing evokes a sense of awe and wonder that speaks to the heart and takes one on their personal journey of self-reflection.

Her study abroad and travels stirred a deeper ap-preciation for the beauty of God's creation that's re-alized in the creative and artsy nature of her being. She elected earliest retirement eligibility from state service to pursue her business ventures that today include LaDecareaux (interior designs), Our Gift Col-lection (hand crafted and specialty gifts), and Wed-ding & All-Occasion Florals.

While multi-talented and gifted, Rose recognizes the responsibility and accountability to service. To this end, her passion and love for God and mankind is ex-emplified in service to God through her local Jackson Revival Center Church, her family and community. She currently serves as Assistant Director of the JRC theatre Ministry of Recollection and Member of the Altar Team Prayer Ministry. She has also had her time of mentoring youth working with the GCC's (a group of young girls) spending summer week-ends teaching cooking and sewing skills and techniques while interjecting Christian principles.

Praise and Worshipper, Dancer, Singer, Musician, Intercessor, Playwright, Poet, Author all capture her expression of service, but simply put, she states, "It's all about the Love of God—Loving Him and allowing Him to love through me."

Contact Information

Email
rosepetalstheauthor@gmail.com

Facebook
rosepetalstheauthor

Instagram
@_rosepetalstheauthor

Online
www.rosepetalstheauthor.com

Phone
(601) 373-7710